The Separation of Church and State

Exploring the Constitution Series

by Darien A. McWhirter

The Separation of Church and State
Freedom of Speech, Press, and Assembly
Search and Seizure
Equal Protection

The Separation of Church and State

by
Darien A. McWhirter

Exploring the Constitution Series
Darien A. McWhirter, Series Editor

Oryx
1994

The rare Arabian Oryx is believed to have inspired the myth of the unicorn. This desert antelope became virtually extinct in the early 1960s. At that time several groups of international conservationists arranged to have 9 animals sent to the Phoenix Zoo to be the nucleus of a captive breeding herd. Today the Oryx population is nearly 800, and over 400 have been returned to reserves in the Middle East.

Copyright © 1994 by Darien A. McWhirter
The Oryx Press
4041 North Central at Indian School Road
Phoenix, Arizona 85012-3397

Published simultaneously in Canada

Printed and Bound in the United States of America

(∞)The paper used in this publication meets the minimum requirements of American National Standard for Information Science—Permanence of Paper for Printed Library Materials, ANSI Z39.48, 1984

This publication is designed to provide accurate and authoritative information in regard to the subject matter covered. It is sold with the understanding that the publisher is not engaged in rendering legal, accounting, or other professional services. If legal advice or other expert assistance is required, the services of a competent professional should be sought.

From a Declaration of Principles jointly adopted by a Committee of the American Bar Association and the Committee of Publishers.

Library of Congress Cataloging-in-Publication Data

McWhirter, Darien A. (Darien Auburn)
The Separation of Church and State/by
Darien McWhirter.
p. cm.—(Exploring the Constitution series)
Includes index.
ISBN 0-89774-852-2 (acid-free paper)
1. Church and state—United States—History.   2. Church and state—United States—Cases.   I. Title.   II. Series.
KF4865.M36   1994
342.73—dc20   93-40703
[3476.302]   CIP

CONTENTS

• • • • • • • •

SERIES STATEMENT

* * * * * * * * *

The Constitution of the United States is one of the most important documents ever written, but it is not just of historical interest. Over two centuries after its adoption, the Constitution continues to influence the lives of everyone in the United States. Many of the most divisive social issues, from abortion to free speech, have been and are being resolved by the U.S. Supreme Court through interpretation of the U.S. Constitution.

Yet much of what has been written about these Supreme Court decisions and the Constitution itself has served only to confuse people who would like to understand exactly what the Court has ruled and exactly what the Constitution means. So much of the discussion revolves around what the Constitution *should* mean that what the Constitution actually *does* mean is obscured.

The Exploring the Constitution Series provides a basic introduction to important areas of constitutional law. While the books in this series are appropriate for a general audience, every effort has been made to ensure that they are especially accessible to high school and college students.

Each volume contains a general introduction to a particular constitutional issue combined with excerpts from significant Supreme Court decisions in that area. The text of the Constitution, a chronological listing of the Supreme Court justices, and a glossary of legal terms are included in each volume. Every effort has been made to provide an objective analysis of the Court's interpretation of constitutional issues with an emphasis on how that interpretation has evolved over time.

PREFACE

• • • • • • • •

No area of constitutional decision making has generated more controversy than the separation of church and state, which includes such issues as prayer in public schools and ritual peyote smoking. The task of maintaining the separation between church and state required by the First Amendment of the U.S. Constitution has kept the Supreme Court busy. As one religious issue appears to leave center stage, another one rises to take its place. In no other area of constitutional debate do both sides bring such emotional commitment to their arguments.

Also, in no other area of constitutional decision making does the Court find itself between two potentially conflicting constitutional demands. The First Amendment demands that the right to freely exercise religion be protected from government interference and that government not establish religion.

PURPOSE

While this volume is written for everyone, every effort has been made to make the discussion interesting and accessible to high school and college students. Issues and Supreme Court decisions have been chosen with an eye to what students might find interesting. Cases involving schools, both public and private, have been included.

This volume is intended to be useful both as a reference work and as a supplement to the standard textbook in social studies, history, religion, government, political science, and law courses. The Supreme Court decisions reprinted here were chosen because of their importance and the likelihood that they would stimulate discussion about the issues presented in this volume. Teachers might consider having students read only the actual Court decisions in preparation for class discussion, and then having students read the discussion material following the class discussion.

In addition to the actual texts of some of the most important Supreme Court decisions in this area, this volume provides the reader with discussions that place those decisions into their legal and historical context. While other sources provide either analysis or the text of actual Court decisions, this volume attempts to provide both in a format that will both stimulate thinking and provide a general overview of the separation of church and state for readers who have little or no background in this important area of constitutional law. Both the discussion and the decisions are necessary for anyone who is really interested in understanding how the Supreme Court has interpreted the religion clauses of the First Amendment. It is assumed, however, that readers have a general understanding of how the American legal system works and the role of the U.S. Supreme Court in that system.

Other sources have discussed some of the material presented here, but such discussions usually present only one side of the separation of church and state debate. This volume attempts to explain as objectively as possible what the Supreme Court has ruled in this area. Supreme Court decisions are criticized here to the extent that they do not logically follow from earlier decisions, not because they fail to live up to the author's personal beliefs about what the Court should rule in this complex area of constitutional law.

ARRANGEMENT

This volume discusses six major separation of church and state issues that the Supreme Court has addressed. Chapters 2, 3, and 4 are primarily concerned with the First Amendment command not to establish religion. Chapter 2 examines the Court's decisions about prayer in public schools and related issues such as Bible reading and the teaching of creation-science in public schools. Chapter 3 examines the complex area of when and how government may provide support for private religious schools. Chapter 4 looks at the use of religious symbols by government, particularly the display of nativity scenes during the Christmas holidays.

Chapters 5, 6, and 7 focus on the First Amendment command to protect the right to freely exercise religion. Chapter 5 explores the right to speak out on religious issues and the right of schoolchildren to refuse to say the Pledge of Allegiance to the American flag in public schools. Chapter 6 looks at issues of conscience, such as when government may exempt conscientious objectors from compulsory military service, and when students may be exempted from compulsory education laws. Chapter 7 examines when people accused of breaking the criminal laws may use their religion as an excuse and avoid punishment.

Each of the six substantive chapters (2 through 7) is divided into three parts. The first part, "Discussion," provides an overview of the important Supreme Court decisions in a particular area to show the development of the Supreme Court's thinking over time. Each of the substantive chapters also contains excerpts from the text of two Supreme Court decisions that illustrate the major issues under discussion and the logic behind the Court's thinking in each area. Discussion questions at the end of each of these chapters are intended to stimulate thought and discussion.

The table of cases provides references to all of the Supreme Court decisions discussed in the text. Anyone wishing to read the actual decisions may find them by showing the reference to a librarian in a library that contains the Supreme Court's decisions. The citation 374 U.S. 203 (1963), for example, tells us that the decision was made in 1963, and that the text of the decision is contained in volume 374 of the United States Reports at page 203.

The glossary is included to provide a ready reference, but students may wish to research some of the terms further. Not every term found in the glossary will be found in each volume of this series.

This volume contains three appendixes. Appendix A contains the complete text of the Constitution. Appendix B contains a chronological listing of all the justices who have sat on the U.S. Supreme Court. Appendix C contains the complete text of the Bill for Establishing Religious Freedom in Virginia. This statute, written by Thomas Jefferson and passed by the Virginia legislature over two centuries ago, has been referred to many times in the two centuries since the Bill of Rights was adopted in an attempt to discover what the authors of the First Amendment intended in the area of religion.

When Thomas Jefferson wrote to the Danbury Baptist Association in an effort to explain his own opinion concerning the relationship between religion and government, he said that he hoped America would be able to build a wall of separation between the church and the state. The Supreme Court has accepted this task and has labored for many decades in an attempt to build and maintain that wall of separation. It is only by reading the Court's actual decisions and understanding the legal and historical context of those decisions that any citizen can begin to understand what the law is in this area and why it is what it is. It is to that end that this volume was written and it is to the education of those citizens that this volume dedicated.

Darien A. McWhirter
San Jose, California
February 1994

TABLE OF CASES CITED IN
THE TEXT

• • • • • • • •

The Separation of
Church and State

CHAPTER
one
•••••••••

Introduction

A discussion of the separation of church and state in the United States is concerned with the meaning of 16 words—two clauses—in the First Amendment to the U.S. Constitution. The First Amendment states that "Congress shall make no law respecting an establishment of religion, or prohibiting the free exercise thereof . . ." The first part of this statement is called the Establishment Clause, and the second is called the Free Exercise Clause. Before we can discuss what these clauses mean today, it is important to consider their history.

EARLY PROPONENTS OF THE SEPARATION OF CHURCH AND STATE

The two philosophers who had the greatest impact on the people who wrote the U.S. Constitution were John Locke and Baron de Montesquieu. Both had written extensively in support of a separation between religion and the state, and their ideas and writings were frequently used to support various positions in the debates about what the Constitution should contain.

John Locke

John Locke was born in England, the son of an attorney, in 1632. Before his death in 1704, he had witnessed the beheading of an English king, Charles I, and a series of civil wars and revolutions in England that changed an absolute monarchy into a democracy. During the English Civil War, while young John attended Puritan schools (including Christ Church College at Oxford University), his father fought for democracy on the side of Oliver Cromwell.

After Cromwell's victory, John Locke witnessed the inability of the three major Protestant sects in England (the Puritans, Anglicans, and Presbyterians) to get along with one another. Their battles over religion contributed to the downfall of the democratic forces and the restoration of the monarch, Charles II. When Charles II died and his brother, James II, took the throne, fear spread that King James, a Catholic, intended to put Catholic officers in the army and in high positions in government. This fear led to the Glorious Revolution in 1688 and the end of James II's reign. In 1689 the crown was offered to William of Orange, but only on the condition that he agree to a bill of rights. This Bill of Rights forbade a Catholic king and prohibited standing armies in time of peace.

After the Glorious Revolution, John Locke was able to publish his political writings, which called for religious toleration. In a free society, Locke argued, people should be free to decide how they will worship. He also asserted that religious intolerance could be a threat to democracy itself, as those who are denied the right to worship as they wish would find revolution to be their only recourse. In his mind, democracy and freedom of religion went hand in hand.

Baron de Montesquieu

Baron de Montesquieu was a Catholic aristocrat in Catholic France (1689–1755). He was born wealthy and then married a wealthy Protestant woman, which assured his fortune. In 1721 he published a book of satire called *The Persian Letters*, which was so successful that it made him a third fortune. In *The Persian Letters*, an imaginary traveler from Persia comments on various aspects of French society. Through these comments, Montesquieu pokes fun at everything, but much of his criticism is aimed at religion. For example, the Persian traveler can not understand a religion that allows people to break their vows and then purchase forgiveness from the bishop. In Letter #85, Montesquieu makes a plea for religious tolerance; in this letter the imaginary Persian points out that having competing religious sects puts everyone on their guard, because no one wants to dishonor his or her own sect in the eyes of the members of the other sects.

Montesquieu also has his traveler say:

> Someone who tries to make me change my religion does so only, I presume, because he would not change his own, even if attempts were made to compel him; so that he finds it strange that I will not do something that he would not do himself, perhaps not even to be ruler of the world.

Montesquieu's great work is *The Spirit of Laws*. In this book he argued that the three branches of government, the judicial, legislative, and executive, should be separated. The authors of the Constitution took his advice on this point when they created the federal government in the United States. He also argued for a separation of religion and the state. He believed that criminal law should not punish thoughts or beliefs, only overt acts, and that only God should punish crimes against religious teachings.

COLONIAL AMERICA

Although the American colonies were populated by many different peoples, most of these people had no desire to establish a system of religious freedom when they first arrived. Rather, they wanted to create a society in which *their* religion would be the only recognized religion. The Puritans, who had fled from England so that they could worship their own way, quickly set up a society in which only Puritans were welcome. More people were executed in seventeenth-century New England for committing the crime of being a Quaker than for any other crime. Different colonies were set up by different religious groups. William Penn founded Pennsylvania as a refuge for Quakers, while Virginia recognized only the Church of England (which later became the Episcopal Church).

Religious Freedom

After the American Revolution, more and more of America's leaders began to argue for religious freedom. In 1784 the Virginia House of Delegates began considering a bill to pay "teachers of the Christian religion." The House decided to postpone consideration of the bill until the next year so that copies of the bill could be published and distributed and the general population could express its opinion on the bill.

James Madison and Thomas Jefferson argued that this bill should not be passed. James Madison wrote a booklet, "Memorial and Remonstrance," in which he argued that religion is not within the "cognizance of civil government." The next year not only was the bill to pay Christian teachers defeated, but another bill, A Bill for Establishing Religious Freedom in Virginia (see appendix C), written by Thomas Jefferson, was passed in its place. This bill put an end to the favored position of the Church of England in Virginia. No longer would tax money be used to build churches and pay ministers. The bill also guaranteed that members of other religions would be able to believe whatever they wished and worship as they saw fit.

The Bill of Rights

In 1787 a convention met to prepare the U.S. Constitution. Thomas Jefferson, because he was minister to France, could not be present at the convention. When he received a copy of the new Constitution, he wrote back that he believed a bill of rights was needed protecting such things as the freedom of religion. Five of the states, while adopting the Constitution, proposed amendments. Three of these states—New Hampshire, New York, and Virginia—

included in their proposals protection for religious freedom. North Carolina at first refused to ratify the Constitution until a bill of rights had been prepared. At the first session of the first Congress, a set of 12 amendments was proposed by James Madison based on the suggestions of the states. These amendments were modified by both the House and the Senate and were then passed as the first 10 amendments to the Constitution. These amendments, what we now refer to as the Bill of Rights, were then ratified by the states.

Soon after the adoption of the Bill of Rights, Thomas Jefferson, in a letter to the Danbury Baptist Association, wrote what may be the most quoted statement concerning the meaning of the religion clauses of the First Amendment. He said:

> Believing with you that religion is a matter which lies solely between man and his God; that he owes account to none other for his faith or his worship; that the legislative powers of the government reach actions only, and not opinions, I contemplate with sovereign reverence that act of the whole American people which declared that their legislature should "make no law respecting an establishment of religion, or prohibiting the free exercise thereof," thus building a wall of separation between church and State. Adhering to this expression of the supreme will of the nation in behalf of the rights of conscience, I shall see with sincere satisfaction the progress of those sentiments which tend to restore man to all of his natural rights, convinced he has no natural right in opposition to his social duties.

Thomas Jefferson's statement that the purpose of the religion clauses was to build "a wall of separation between church and State" has been quoted many times by the members of the U.S. Supreme Court over the last two centuries as they have tried to apply the religion clauses to concrete situations. Chief Justice Waite, writing for a unanimous Court in the 1878 decision in *Reynolds v. United States* (see p. 120), declared that this statement by Thomas Jefferson "may be accepted almost as an authoritative declaration of the scope and effect of the" religion clauses of the First Amendment.

THE TWO HORNS OF A DILEMMA

The two religion clauses have always presented the Supreme Court with two horns of a dilemma. There is tension between the requirements of the Establishment Clause and the requirements of the Free Exercise Clause. If the Court goes too far to prevent the "establishment of religion," it risks interfering with the free exercise of religion, which violates the Free Exercise Clause. On the other hand, if the Court goes too far to protect the right of free exercise of religion, that might be seen as an attempt to aid one religion or all religions, which would violate the Establishment Clause.

While we can disagree with some of the Court's decisions, it is important to realize how difficult these decisions have been to make. In no other area of constitutional decision making is the Court faced with such potentially conflicting commands. If the Court goes too far to protect the right of free speech, for example, it may be causing an inconvenience for those who have to listen, but it does not risk violating some other section of the Constitution.

In trying to make decisions about the separation of church and state, the Supreme Court has come up with a variety of "tests" and decision rules, which it has then added to, modified, or abandoned over time. Each particular problem has required a new look at both the Establishment Clause and the Free Exercise Clause. In the next six chapters, we will look at six major problems that the Court has faced.

The Establishment Clause

The Establishment Clause prohibits the creation of a national church. The difficult question has been to what extent it prohibits government support for religion. Chapter 2 looks at prayer in public schools. Chapter 3 discusses the question of how much support government can give to private religious schools without violating the Establishment Clause. Chapter 4 examines when governments may use religious symbols, and in particular, when governments may display Christian nativity scenes without violating the Establishment Clause.

The Free Exercise Clause

The Free Exercise Clause clearly guarantees everyone the right to believe whatever they want to believe when it comes to religion. The difficult question has been to what extent the Free Exercise Clause protects actions as well as beliefs.

Chapter 5 examines two Supreme Court decisions handed down in 1940 and 1943 concerning the right of students to refuse to say the Pledge of Allegiance to the American flag, and looks at other cases concerned with the right to speak or not speak about issues related to religion. Chapter 6 deals with the issue of whether or not parents have the right to send their children to private religious schools instead of public schools and the extent to which people may be exempted from military service because of their religious beliefs. Chapter 7 examines the extent to which religious people acting on their religious beliefs may violate the criminal law and avoid prosecution. Chapter 8 summarizes the Supreme Court's rulings in the area of separation of church and state, and asks whether these rulings are consistent with one another.

CONSTITUTIONAL DECISION MAKING

The U.S. Supreme Court has developed a number of approaches to use in making decisions about constitutional provisions. The justices may use one, or more than one, approach in any one case. First, they may try to figure out what the authors of a particular provision had in mind when they wrote it. This approach is difficult to use with the Bill of Rights, because the amendments that make up the Bill of Rights were voted on not only by Congress, but also by the many state legislatures, and it is not easy to find out what all of those people had in mind when they cast their votes. At the same time, it can be useful to look at how some church and state issues were handled soon after the Bill of Rights was added to the Constitution. In this way, the Court may get some idea of what the people who voted for the Bill of Rights thought it required of them.

Second, constitutional decision making often involves drawing a line. The Court decides that one type of behavior is protected from governmental interference by a particular provision of the Bill of Rights, and another type of behavior is not. For example, in the 1920s the Supreme Court said that the right of free speech includes the right to criticize the actions of the president of the United States but not the right to yell "Fire!" in a crowded theater.

Third, constitutional decision making often involves trying to balance government goals against individual rights. In evaluating a case, the Court must weigh the importance of the goals government is trying to achieve by passing a particular law or by engaging in a particular action against the damage the law or action appears to do to the individual rights of the citizens. For example, when San Francisco was burning down after the great earthquake of 1906, the government blew up people's houses in an effort to stop the spread of the fire. Generally government is not allowed to destroy people's houses, but in this case the need was very great, so this government action was allowed. Often the Supreme Court asks how "compelling" is the goal government is trying to achieve. Then the Court tries to balance that against the importance of the right that is being infringed upon.

THE SUPREME COURT OVER TIME

In reading about decisions handed down by the U.S. Supreme Court over the last two centuries, it is important to realize that during those two centuries American society evolved significantly. What began as a very rural society, made up mainly of small farmers, became a very urban society, with most people working in commerce or industry. A very homogeneous society, made up mainly of Protestants, became a very heterogeneous society, with residents coming from every corner of the globe, representing almost every religion on earth.

Generally people divide the history of the U.S. Supreme Court into three major eras: before the Civil War, between the Civil War and the Great Depression, and the modern era. The modern era can be broken up further into the New Deal Court (1941–53), the Warren Court (1953–69), the Burger Court (1969–86), and the Rehnquist Court (1986–present).

Pre-Civil War to the Great Depression

Before the Civil War, the Supreme Court spent very little time on the meaning of the Bill of Rights. The Court decided that the Bill of Rights restricted only the federal government. State and local governments were free to do whatever they wanted, limited only by the bills of rights contained in state constitutions. Most of the governmental activities that touched people's lives were carried on by state governments, not by the federal government.

The Civil War was a great turning point in American history. With the victory of the Union army, two fundamental questions that had not been answered by the Constitution were well on their way to resolution. These were the question of the extent of the federal government's power to control the states, and the question of slavery. After the Civil War, in the partnership between the states and the federal government, the federal government would be the more powerful partner, and slavery would be abolished in the United States. The Thirteenth, Fourteenth, and Fifteenth Amendments were then passed to make it clear to future generations who had won the Civil War and what should follow from that victory.

Between the Civil War and the Great Depression, the Supreme Court struggled to decide what these three amendments actually meant; the key question for the Court was the meaning of the Fourteenth Amendment. The Court decided that the amendment protected basic liberties of all Americans from infringement by state and local governments, but this raised another difficult question: What were the basic liberties that were protected? Between the Civil War and the Great Depression, the Court refused to be specific about this question. It simply took each case as it came, and decided whether or not the freedoms involved were important enough to protect with the Fourteenth Amendment.

Critics of the Court argued that the members of the Court were simply using the Fourteenth Amendment as an excuse to overturn laws passed by the state legislatures because a majority of the justices did not agree with the laws, not because the laws violated any particular right. From the 1880s to the 1930s, 200 statutes were overturned by the Court. Most of these statutes attempted to regulate industry. For example, the Court overturned a New York law that limited bakers to a 60-hour work week. Other laws declared unconstitutional had attempted to protect a worker's right to join a labor union. While the Court argued that it was protecting the right of workers to work more than 60 hours a week and to not join labor unions, critics argued that the Court was mainly protecting the right of employers to exploit their employees.

The Modern Era

Beginning in the 1930s, the Court began to move away from this expansive idea and to develop the concept that the Fourteenth Amendment actually made most of the federal Bill of Rights applicable to state and local government. This countered the critics and enabled the Court to give real substance to the Fourteenth Amendment's command that everyone should be able to enjoy liberty in the United States.

At the same time, the composition of the Court was changing. By 1941 eight of the justices had been appointed by President Roosevelt. What had been a conservative court dominated by Republicans became a liberal court dominated by Democrats, the New Deal Court. As a practical matter, this meant that the Court spent less time trying to protect business from government, and more time trying to protect the rights of individuals and minority groups.

In 1953 President Eisenhower appointed Earl Warren as chief justice of the Supreme Court, and in 1956 Eisenhower appointed William Brennan associate justice. These two justices turned out to be as concerned with the rights of individuals and minorities as the New Deal Court had been. The period from 1953 to 1969 is known as the Warren era in Supreme Court history, and many difficult issues concerning the meaning of the Bill of Rights and the relative power of the state and federal governments were decided during that time by the Warren Court.

In 1969 President Nixon appointed Warren Burger as chief justice; Burger was replaced by William Rehnquist in 1986. During this period, through the Burger Court and the Rehnquist Court, the Supreme Court is generally considered to have moved in a more conservative direction. That does not mean that the decisions of the New Deal and Warren Courts were simply overturned—far from it—but the tone and direction of the Court did change. The interests of the state and federal government were given greater emphasis, along with the needs of business.

Although the direction of the Court may change over time with the addition of new justices, the Court is limited by the doctrine of *stare decisis*. This is a Latin phrase meaning "the decision must stand." In the American legal system, it means that generally a past decision of the Supreme Court will not be overturned except under exceptional circumstances.

In the area of religion, the political and ideological affiliation of the justices has not determined how they have voted. For example, in the first decision about aid to religious schools, handed down in 1947, all of the justices were liberal Democrats, yet the Court divided five to four over the decision. The five-member majority decided that New Jersey would be allowed to provide free bus transportation to students attending Catholic school. In 1992, in the most recent prayer in public schools case, eight of the justices were conservative Republicans, yet five of these conservative Republicans voted to maintain the ban on prayer in the public schools.

What has been true of the Court has also been true of American society in general. The members of some religions have been in favor of prayer in public schools, while others have been against it. The members of some religious groups would like to see government provide as much financial aid to private religious schools as possible, while other religious sects oppose this use of public funds.

CONCLUSION

This book discusses the most difficult and divisive area of constitutional decision making—the separation of church and state. However, those of us who approach this issue today have the benefit of both hindsight and over a century of Supreme Court decisions on the subject. We can also see what questions and problems have resulted from particular decisions that could not have been anticipated by the justices who made those early decisions.

No group of Supreme Court decisions has generated as much controversy as the decisions discussed here. When six of the nine justices voted to outlaw prayer in public schools in 1962, millions urged Congress to impeach the then chief justice, Earl Warren. While the Court generally tries to ignore public sentiment when making constitutional decisions, that has been impossible in this area.

In no other area of constitutional decision making have so many justices changed their minds over time. This is best exemplified by the change from 1940 to 1943 on the issue of allowing schools to expel children for refusing to say the Pledge of Allegiance to the American flag. During a span of only three years, three justices changed their minds and the 1940 decision was overruled. Other justices have changed their minds when a decision is seen years later to have unexpected results.

There is a tendency in the popular press to caricature some members of the Supreme Court or to question their integrity. That is unfair. Even if we disagree with the stand taken by a particular justice, we must never lose sight of the fact that he or she is trying to live up to the greatest tradition of judicial integrity in history. Much more is to be gained by trying to understand the position of both sides than by dismissing the opinions of these justices as either personal bias or political expediency.

No matter what a person's opinions are concerning the proper line of separation between church and state, it is important to understand what the Court has ruled in this area and why. Disagreement based on ignorance is worthless. Reasoned argument based on understanding and facts is the most powerful weapon anyone can wield in a free society.

CHAPTER
two
•••••••••

Prayer in Public Schools

•••••••••••••••••••••••••••••• DISCUSSION •••••••••••••••••••••••••••••••

When the members of the first Congress passed the First Amendment (and sent it to the states for ratification), they voted to prohibit the "establishment" of religion. Since at that time many of the states, and most foreign countries, had an established church, it is assumed that these first congressional representatives intended to prevent a future Congress or president from declaring that only one church could exist in the United States. The question that has been left to later generations has been: What else is prohibited by this part of the First Amendment?

Over time it was generally accepted that the First Amendment prohibited federal, state, or local governments in the United States from raising tax money for a church, or for a particular group of churches. In many foreign countries, citizens still must declare each year what church they belong to, and tax money that they pay to the government is then forwarded to their religion. This would clearly be unconstitutional in the United States.

Eventually the Supreme Court said that the Establishment Clause requires government to be "neutral" with regard to religion. Government may not favor one religion over other religions, or favor religion over nonreligion. There must be a wall of separation between church and state. The challenge for the Court has been to determine just how high that wall must be.

OFFICIAL PRAYERS IN PUBLIC SCHOOLS

In 1962 the U.S. Supreme Court had to face a very difficult question. Does the Establishment Clause of the First Amendment prevent public schools from having prayers? This case, *Engel v. Vitale* (see p. 20), involved a prayer published by the New York Board of Regents. This prayer, which was recited by public school teachers and schoolchildren at the beginning of the school day in many New York public schools, said: "Almighty God, we acknowledge our dependence upon Thee, and we beg Thy blessings upon us, our parents, our teachers and our Country." Students were allowed to leave the room if they did not want to participate in saying this prayer.

Some parents objected that their children were forced to hear this "official" prayer in a public school. They believed that having an official prayer clearly showed that the New York public schools were not neutral on the issue of religion. They argued that because this prayer was to "Almighty God," it clearly showed support for those religions that believe in one almighty God. This in turn suggested that the state of New York did not support other religions that require people to pray in a different way or to a different god or gods.

The state of New York argued that America was founded upon the belief in one almighty God. While America tolerates those who believe differently, the state of New York argued that it should have the right to acknowledge this belief in its public schools. The prayer in question was not a Catholic or Protestant prayer, just a general prayer asking for the blessing of God.

Critics of school prayer argued that some of the students belonged to non-Christian religions and this prayer was offensive to them. The critics also believed that it would be impossible to have a prayer that would not offend someone. While there might have been a time two centuries ago when everyone in the United States could be considered a Christian, that was no longer the case. In the twentieth century in the United States, almost every religion on earth is represented.

The real issue of this first prayer in the public schools case was whether or not having such a prayer constituted "establishing" a religion. Six of the nine justices on the Supreme Court agreed that it did (two justices did not take part in this decision). Justice Black, who wrote the majority opinion, stated that reciting an official prayer in a public school was too much like holding a religious service for children who are forced to attend. In the opinion of the majority, forced attendance at a government-sponsored religious service violated the Establishment Clause of the First Amendment.

The state of New York argued that not allowing an official school prayer amounted to government hostility toward religion. Justice Black did not agree; he thought that the state should be neutral with regard to different religions, and with regard to religion in general. Having children in public school recite the official prayer prevented the state from being neutral with regard to religion and showed official support for a particular group of religions.

BIBLE READINGS

In 1963 the Court came to a similar conclusion. This case, *Abington School District v. Schempp*, involved the state of Pennsylvania, which had passed a law requiring that at least 10 verses of the Bible be read in public schools each day. In most schools, the 10 verses were read over the public-address system. As in *Engel v. Vitale*, students who objected to this practice could ask to be excused from the room while this was being done. Eight of the justices thought that this practice violated the Establishment Clause. The justices ruled that reading Bible verses would create an identification in the minds of the students between the state and a particular religious text, the Bible.

It is important to realize that these Bible verses were not being read along with material from other religious books as part of a class in the religions of the world. The verses were being read over the public-address system every day to impress upon the students that they should follow the teachings of the Bible. Justice Clark, writing for the majority, pointed out that it would be permissible to read the Bible in a history or religion class that looked at the Bible as one of many religious texts. The problem in the *Schempp* case was that the state of Pennsylvania was clearly endorsing a particular religion.

The state of Pennsylvania argued that students were free to leave the room while the verses were being read. Given the reality of most classroom situations, however, the justices didn't think that children would really be free to leave. The Court believed that most students would be afraid to ask to be excused, for fear it would damage their relationship with the teacher or with fellow students.

Justice Clark said that the test of whether or not something violates the Establishment Clause should be whether or not the practice would advance religion in general or one religion in particular. He thought that reading Bible verses advanced those religions that held the Bible to be a sacred book.

Critics of the Court argued that reading the Bible verses was a very small violation of the principle that church and state should be kept separate. Justice Clark answered them by saying that what is a "trickling stream" today may become a "raging torrent" tomorrow if left unchecked. This is a common way for judges to look at a problem. They often have to draw the line between what is acceptable and what is not. Once the Court decides that one type of behavior is constitutional, it will have to decide whether other types of similar behavior are also constitutional. This is often difficult to do.

The state of Pennsylvania argued that by outlawing the reading of Bible verses, the Court was showing hostility to religion. Justice Clark did not agree. He stated that, although it would be unconstitutional for a state to show favoritism for a religion, as Pennsylvania was doing in this case, it would be also be unconstitutional for a state to show positive hostility to a religion.

Justice Stewart, the lone dissenter, argued that not allowing public schools to read Bible verses to the schoolchildren who wanted to hear them was an interference with the students' right of religious freedom. He did not think that the reading of Bible verses would actually force anyone to change their religious beliefs, and therefore did not constitute a violation of the Establishment Clause.

Lawyers and judges often reason through a decision by asking how a decision might come out if the facts were changed but the legal principle remained the same. In this case, we could imagine a school district in which the majority of the citizens were Satan worshipers and the school board demanded that each day the students recite a prayer to Satan. Most Americans would find this prayer unacceptable. But the argument can be made that if prayers to God are constitutional in public schools, then prayers to Satan must also be constitutional.

The principle that came out of the decisions in *Engel v. Vitale* and *Abington School District v. Schempp* is that government has to be neutral when it comes to different religions. It cannot be seen to support some religions against other religions.

These two decisions generated a great deal of criticism. Many people, particularly some Christians, believed that the United States was founded by Christians, and that it should be acceptable for schools to reflect that. While these people acknowledged that the Establishment Clause prevented spending tax money on churches, they did not believe that a short prayer or Bible reading in public school violated the Establishment Clause.

EVOLUTION

The 1968 case of *Epperson v. Arkansas* concerned an Arkansas law that forbade the teaching of evolution in Arkansas public schools. The law specifically said that a public school teacher could not teach that human beings "ascended or descended" from animals. The case had been brought by a biology teacher who wanted to teach evolution in her biology class. After the Arkansas Supreme Court upheld this law, ruling that the state of Arkansas had the power to control the curriculum of the public schools of Arkansas, the case was appealed to the U.S. Supreme Court. A unanimous Supreme Court ruled that this Arkansas law violated the Establishment Clause.

Before the U.S. Supreme Court, the state of Arkansas argued that the public schools belonged to the state, and it was up to the state to decide what would be taught in those schools. The Supreme Court justices did not agree. While in general it is up to the state to decide what the public school curriculum should be, the state can not make that decision based on religion. The Court concluded that in this case, the state had outlawed the teaching of evolution because it conflicted with a "particular religious doctrine." If Pennsylvania could not require the reading of the Bible (*Abington School District v. Schempp*), then Arkansas could not prevent the teaching of evolution. In both cases, the justices believed, the motivation behind the laws was religious, and because of this the laws violated the Establishment Clause.

Justice Fortas, writing for a unanimous Court, ruled that government may not "aid, foster or promote one religious theory" over others; government must be neutral between religious sects, and between the religious and the nonreligious. States may not require that teaching be tailored to the principles of a particular religious sect.

POSTING THE TEN COMMANDMENTS

In 1980, with the case of *Stone v. Graham*, the Supreme Court was faced with a Kentucky law that required public schools to post the Ten Commandments in every classroom. The actual pieces of paper on which the Ten Commandments were printed were paid for with voluntary contributions, not tax dollars. There was no recitation of the Ten Commandments by the teacher each day. The Ten Commandments were simply posted in each classroom for the children to see.

The state of Kentucky argued that the Ten Commandments were posted simply as a guide for the children concerning what they should and should not do, rather than as support for a particular religion. A majority of the justices thought that the Ten Commandments are clearly "religious" in nature and a sacred text of the Jewish and Christian faiths. By posting the Ten Commandments, the Court ruled, the state of Kentucky was showing support for a particular group of religions.

The Ten Commandments were not posted along with similar statements from other religions concerning what kinds of behavior people should engage in, or as part of a class in history or comparative religion. The Court believed that simply posting the Ten Commandments in every classroom indicated to the children that the government supported a particular group of religions to the exclusion of other religions. This was a violation of the Establishment Clause. The Ten Commandments could of course be read by the students and discussed as part of a discussion of history, civilization, ethics, or religion.

The state of Kentucky argued that the fact that the actual pieces of paper with the Ten Commandments printed on them were not purchased with public funds, along with the fact that the Ten Commandments were simply posted on the wall and not read aloud, should make a difference. The Court did not agree. Regardless of who paid for the pieces of paper, and regardless of whether or not the Ten Commandments were read aloud or simply posted on the wall, the Court believed that having them there was a clear endorsement of a particular group of religions by government.

PRAYER IN LEGISLATURES

In 1983, with the case of *Marsh v. Chambers*, the Supreme Court had to rule on a related question. Most legislatures and the U.S. Congress have a chaplain, paid with government funds, who recites a prayer to begin each day of the legislative session. The question for the Court was: Does the recitation of an official prayer each day in Congress or in a state capitol violate the Establishment Clause?

Chief Justice Burger, writing for the majority of the justices in this six-to-three decision, ruled that this practice was not a violation of the Establishment Clause. He pointed out that the same Congress that voted to place the First Amendment into the Constitution over two centuries ago also began every day with a prayer from a chaplain. If the members of that Congress had intended the Establishment Clause to outlaw this kind of behavior, surely they would have stopped this practice once the First Amendment went into effect. They did not. Therefore, they must not have intended the First Amendment to outlaw this kind of practice.

Chief Justice Burger also emphasized that the legislators listening to this prayer were adults, not young schoolchildren. He did not feel that adults would be swayed by the prayer. He argued that, unlike children, these adults would not be "readily susceptible to religious indoctrination" or peer pressure to behave differently or believe differently. In a sense, the chief justice seemed to be saying that the prayer was simply part of the formal procedure of beginning the legislative day, and that no one really paid much attention to it. Because the prayer was not really an attempt to change anyone's mind about religion, it was not unconstitutional.

Chief Justice Burger also did not think that the fact that the chaplain was paid with public funds violated the Establishment Clause. Again, the chaplains of the U.S. Congress were paid with public funds two centuries ago, and no one who wrote the First Amendment had objected to this practice. He believed that this practice was "deeply embedded in the history and tradition of this country" and should not be changed by the Supreme Court.

Three justices dissented, arguing that an official prayer was an official prayer, regardless of where it was said or who was listening to it. These justices strongly believed that any kind of official prayer violated the First Amendment whether those listening were adult legislators or schoolchildren. They also felt that just because something had been going on for two centuries, that was no reason not to review it in light of the current view about the separation of church and state.

A MOMENT OF SILENCE

In 1985, with a six-to-three decision in the case of *Wallace v. Jaffree*, the Supreme Court overturned a law passed by the Alabama legislature that required a moment of silence at the beginning of each day in the public schools to be used for "meditation or voluntary prayer." A majority of the justices asked whether there was a nonreligous purpose to this law. They could not find one. In fact, the Alabama legislators who proposed this law said that they did so in an attempt to bring prayers back into the public schools. Because the legislators plainly stated that their only reason for passing the law was to attempt to get around the U.S. Supreme Court's decision outlawing prayer in the public schools (*Engel v. Vitale*), the Court believed there was nothing it could do except declare the law to be unconstitutional. The Court had said on many occasions that laws must not have only a religious purpose. In this case, there was no argument from Alabama that there was any secular purpose in requiring the moment of silence.

Justice O'Connor pointed out in her concurring opinion that nothing in the Constitution prevents public school students from "voluntarily praying at any time before, during or after the schoolday." She agreed with the majority that Alabama's statute had been enacted solely to encourage prayer and therefore was unconstitutional. She also argued that a state legislature could pass a law requiring a "moment of silence" without violating the Constitution if the legislature did not suggest that the time should be spent praying. Also, teachers must be careful not to suggest that the time be spent praying. Nevertheless a child could certainly use the time to pray, and in fact the right of a child to pray silently in school is protected by the Free Exercise Clause of the First Amendment.

EQUAL TREATMENT FOR CREATION-SCIENCE

In 1987, with the case of *Edwards v. Aguillard*, the Court was faced with a Louisiana law that required that "creation-science" be given equal treatment if evolution was being taught in a public school. Again, a majority of the justices could not find a secular purpose for this law. Its primary purpose was to advance a particular belief, grounded in religion, that humans did not evolve from lower animals but were placed on the earth in the form we see today by a supreme being.

Writing for the seven-justice majority, Justice Brennan emphasized that parents place their children in public schools in the belief that those children will not be subjected to religious indoctrination that might conflict with what they are being taught at home or in their own church. He noted that the state of Louisiana forces children to attend school. Children who attend public school see their teachers as role models and are very susceptible to peer pressure. As a result, Justice Brennan argued, schoolchildren who did not agree with the creationist point of view would be afraid to speak up.

The majority of justices also believed that the main purpose of the Louisiana law was to further the teachings of a particular group of religions. In the majority opinion, Justice Brennan stated that the main purpose of the "Louisiana legislature was clearly to advance the religious viewpoint that a supernatural being created humankind."

In his dissenting opinion, Justice Scalia, joined by Chief Justice Rehnquist, noted that Louisiana's Balanced Treatment Act forbade the teaching of either "creation-science" or "evolution-science" without instruction in the other. He argued that the term "creation-science" simply refers to the scientific evidence for the proposition that life "appeared suddenly" and had not "changed substantially since appearing." He argued that the Balanced Treatment Act did not require the presentation of religious doctrine. The other seven justices did not agree that "creation-science" could be separated from religion, and specifically from the religions that took the content of the Book of Genesis to be literal truth.

PRAYER AT PUBLIC SCHOOL GRADUATION CEREMONIES

Finally, in 1992, with the case of *Lee v. Weisman* (see p. 24), the Court was forced to draw an even more distinct line between what is constitutional and what is unconstitutional. The case involved the practice in Providence, Rhode Island, of having a short prayer at the beginning and end of public school graduation ceremonies (an invocation and a benediction). The audience at these ceremonies was made up primarily of students and parents. The Court had to decide whether this short prayer was like the prayers recited to open legislative sessions (merely a formality that no one really pays any attention to), or like the daily prayers in public school in front of impressionable schoolchildren (which carry the message that the government supports a particular religion). This was not an easy decision to make.

Four justices thought that the prayers at public school graduation ceremonies were more in the nature of a formality at a public event. These justices believed that the prayers were part of a long tradition, like prayers at legislative sessions, and could not be seen as an attempt to indoctrinate children in a particular religious belief.

The other five justices did not agree and ruled that such prayers violate the Establishment Clause of the First Amendment. Justice Kennedy, who wrote the majority opinion, held that while attendance at public school graduation ceremonies is not required, few students would want to miss the ceremony. While the children could absent themselves from the part of the ceremony that contained the prayer, that would be difficult for them because of the very nature of the graduation process. There would also be peer pressure to participate and to not "make a fuss" about the prayer. The Court ruled that because the graduation ceremony is part of an official public school event, prayers cannot be allowed.

CONCLUSION

Throughout the decades since the first prayer in public school decision was handed down in 1962 (*Engel v. Vitale*), there has been a great deal of debate in the United States concerning whether or not this decision should be overturned. Those who argue that prayers should be allowed in public schools claim that the United States was founded by Christians, and that having a Christian prayer simply reflects that heritage. They point out that children would be free to leave during the prayers, and the prayers would take only a minute during the school day.

People who believe that the Supreme Court was right to outlaw prayers in public schools argue that children would not really be free to leave during the prayer because of peer pressure. These people also question whether government should be allowed to show support for a particular religion in this way.

Presidents Reagan and Bush appointed justices to the Supreme Court who were considered to be more conservative. Many people believed that these justices might overturn the *Engel v. Vitale* decision, but that has not happened. With the 1992 decision in the case of *Lee v. Weisman*, a majority of the justices reaffirmed the principle that prayers are generally not allowed at public schools.

This issue of prayer in public schools has divided even the members of some religious groups. Many are bothered by the question of what such a prayer should contain. Another concern is that if a Christian majority in one school district can force children to pray to Jesus, then in theory a Satanic majority in another district could require children to pray to Satan. Over the course of three decades, a majority of the justices of the Supreme Court have agreed that official prayers in public school raise too many problems. Not only do prayers suggest government endorsement of some religions and amount to a kind of religious indoctrination of schoolchildren, but they also can be seen as an attack on the religious freedom of those children who do not agree with the views expressed in the official prayer.

CASE DECISIONS

The first prayer in the public schools decision was *Engel v. Vitale*, decided in 1962. Justice Black wrote the decision for the majority, which is included here. Justices Frankfurter and White did not take part in the decision. Justice Douglas wrote a concurring opinion, which is not included. Justice Stewart was the only dissenter, and he wrote a dissenting opinion, which is included here. *Engel v. Vitale* was concerned with whether or not the state of New York could have teachers say a prayer each day in the public schools. The Supreme Court ruled that this violated the Establishment Clause of the First Amendment.

The most recent prayer in the public schools case, *Lee v. Weisman*, was decided in 1992. Justice Kennedy wrote the opinion for the five-justice majority, which is included here. Justices Blackmun and Souter wrote concurring opinions, and Justice Scalia wrote a dissenting opinion; these opinions are also included. This case involved the saying of an invocation and a benediction at public school graduation exercises. The five-member majority ruled that this also violated the Establishment Clause of the First Amendment.

Following are excerpts from the case decisions.

* * * * * * * * * *

ENGEL v. VITALE
370 U.S. 421 (1962)

MR. JUSTICE BLACK delivered the opinion of the Court.

The respondent Board of Education of Union Free School District No. 9, New Hyde Park, New York, acting in its official capacity under state law, directed the School District's principal to cause the following prayer to be said aloud by each class in the presence of a teacher at the beginning of each school day:

> "Almighty God, we acknowledge our dependence upon Thee, and we beg
> Thy blessings upon us, our parents, our teachers and our Country."

This daily procedure was adopted on the recommendation of the State Board of Regents, a governmental agency created by the State Constitution to which the New York Legislature has granted broad supervisory, executive, and legislative powers over the State's public school system. These state officials composed the prayer which they recommended and published as a part of their "Statement on Moral and Spiritual Training in the Schools," saying: "We believe that this Statement will be subscribed to by all men and women of good will, and we call upon all of them to aid in giving life to our program."

Shortly after the practice of reciting the Regents' prayer was adopted by the School District, the parents of ten pupils brought this action in a New York

State Court insisting that use of this official prayer in the public schools was contrary to the beliefs, religions, or religious practices of both themselves and their children. Among other things, these parents challenged the constitutionality of both the state law authorizing the School District to direct the use of prayer in public schools and the School District's regulation ordering the recitation of this particular prayer on the ground that these actions of official governmental agencies violate that part of the First Amendment of the Federal Constitution which commands that "Congress shall make no law respecting an establishment of religion"—a command which was "made applicable to the State of New York by the Fourteenth Amendment of the said Constitution." The New York Court of Appeals, over the dissents of Judges Dye and Fuld, sustained an order of the lower state courts which had upheld the power of New York to use the Regents' prayer as a part of the daily procedures of its public schools so long as the schools did not compel any pupil to join in the prayer over his or her parents' objection. . . .

We think that by using its public school system to encourage recitation of the Regents' prayer, the State of New York has adopted a practice wholly inconsistent with the Establishment Clause. There can, of course, be no doubt that New York's program of daily classroom invocation of God's blessings as prescribed in the Regents' prayer is a religious activity. It is a solemn avowal of divine faith and supplication for the blessings of the Almighty. The nature of such a prayer has always been religious, none of the respondents has denied this and the trial court expressly so found:

> "The religious nature of prayer was recognized by Jefferson and has been concurred in by theological writers, the United States Supreme Court and State courts and administrative officials, including New York's Commissioner of Education. A committee of the New York Legislature has agreed.
> "The Board of Regents as *amicus curiae*, the respondents and intervenors all concede the religious nature of prayer, but seek to distinguish this prayer because it is based on our spiritual heritage . . . . "

The petitioners contend among other things that the state laws requiring or permitting use of the Regents' prayer must be struck down as a violation of the Establishment Clause because that prayer was composed by governmental officials as a part of a governmental program to further religious beliefs. For this reason, petitioners argue, the State's use of the Regents' prayer in its public school system breaches the constitutional wall of separation between Church and State. We agree with that contention since we think that the constitutional prohibition against laws respecting an establishment of religion must at least mean that in this country it is no part of the business of government to compose official prayers for any group of the American people to recite as a part of a religious program carried on by government. . . .

It is an unfortunate fact of history that when some of the very groups which had most strenuously opposed the established Church of England found themselves sufficiently in control of colonial governments in this country to write their own prayers into law, they passed laws making their own religion the official religion of their respective colonies. Indeed, as late as the time of the Revolutionary War, there were established churches in at least eight of the thirteen former colonies and established religions in at least four of the other five. But the successful Revolution against English political domination was shortly followed by intense opposition to the practice of establishing religion by law. This opposition crystallized rapidly into an effective political force in Virginia where the minority religious groups such as Presbyterians, Lutherans, Quakers and Baptists had gained such strength that the adherents to the established Episcopal Church were actually a minority themselves. In 1785–1786, those opposed to the established Church, led by James Madison and Thomas Jefferson, who, though themselves not members of any of these dissenting religious groups, opposed all religious establishments by law on grounds of principle, obtained the enactment of the famous "Virginia Bill for Religious Liberty" by which all religious groups were placed on an equal footing so far as the State was concerned. Similar though less far-reaching legislation was being considered and passed in other States. . . .

It has been argued that to apply the Constitution in such a way as to prohibit state laws respecting an establishment of religious services in public schools is to indicate a hostility toward religion or toward prayer. Nothing, of course, could be more wrong. The history of man is inseparable from the history of religion. And perhaps it is not too much to say that since the beginning of that history many people have devoutly believed that "More things are wrought by prayer than this world dreams of." It was doubtless largely due to men who believed this that there grew up a sentiment that caused men to leave the cross-currents of officially established state religions and religious persecution in Europe and come to this country filled with the hope that they could find a place in which they could pray when they pleased to the God of their faith in the language they chose. And there were men of this same faith in the power of prayer who led the fight for adoption of our Constitution and also for our Bill of Rights with the very guarantees of religious freedom that forbid the sort of governmental activity which New York has attempted here. These men knew that the First Amendment, which tried to put an end to governmental control of religion and of prayer, was not written to destroy either. They knew rather that it was written to quiet well-justified fears which nearly all of them felt arising out of an awareness that governments of the past had shackled men's tongues to make them speak only the religious thoughts that government wanted them to speak and to pray only to the God that government wanted them to pray to. It is neither sacrilegious nor antireligious to say that each separate government in this country should stay out of the business of writing or sanctioning official prayers and leave that purely religious function to the people themselves and to those the people choose to look to for religious guidance.

It is true that New York's establishment of its Regents' prayer as an officially approved religious doctrine of that State does not amount to a total establishment of one particular religious sect to the exclusion of all others—that, indeed, the governmental endorsement of that prayer seems relatively insignificant when compared to the governmental encroachments upon religion which were commonplace 200 years ago. To those who may subscribe to the view that because the Regents' official prayer is so brief and general there can be no danger to religious freedom in its governmental establishment, however, it may be appropriate to say in the words of James Madison, the author of the First Amendment:

> "[I]t is proper to take alarm at the first experiment on our liberties.... Who does not see that the same authority which can establish Christianity, in exclusion of all other Religions, may establish with the same ease any particular sect of Christians, in exclusion of all other Sects? That the same authority which can force a citizen to contribute three pence only of his property for the support of any one establishment, may force him to conform to any other establishment in all cases whatsoever?"

The judgment of the Court of Appeals of New York is reversed and the cause remanded for further proceedings not inconsistent with this opinion.

Reversed and remanded.

Dissenting Opinion   MR. JUSTICE STEWART, dissenting.

A local school board in New York has provided that those pupils who wish to do so may join in a brief prayer at the beginning of each school day, acknowledging their dependence upon God and asking His blessing upon them and upon their parents, their teachers, and their country. The Court today decides that in permitting this brief nondenominational prayer the school board has violated the Constitution of the United States. I think this decision is wrong.

The Court does not hold, nor could it, that New York has interfered with the free exercise of anybody's religion. For the state courts have made clear that those who object to reciting the prayer must be entirely free of any compulsion to do so, including any "embarrassments and pressures." Cf. *West Virginia State Board of Education v. Barnette*, 319 U.S. 624. But the Court says that in permitting school children to say this simple prayer, the New York authorities have established "an official religion."

With all respect, I think the Court has misapplied a great constitutional principle. I cannot see how an "official religion" is established by letting those who want to say a prayer say it. On the contrary, I think that to deny the wish of these school children to join in reciting this prayer is to deny them the opportunity of sharing in the spiritual heritage of our Nation. . . .

At the opening of each day's Session of this Court we stand, while one of our officials invokes the protection of God. Since the days of John Marshall our Crier has said "God save the United States and this Honorable Court." Both the Senate and the House of Representatives open their daily Sessions with prayer. Each of our Presidents, from George Washington to John F. Kennedy, has upon assuming his Office asked the protection and help of God. . . .

I do not believe that this Court, or the Congress, or the President has by the actions and practices I have mentioned established an "official religion" in violation of the Constitution. And I do not believe the State of New York has done so in this case. What each has done has been to recognize and to follow the deeply entrenched and highly cherished spiritual traditions of our Nation—traditions which come down to us from those who almost two hundred years ago avowed their "firm Reliance on the Protection of divine Providence" when they proclaimed the freedom and independence of this brave new world.

I dissent.

LEE v. WEISMAN
112 S. Ct. 2649 (1992)

JUSTICE KENNEDY delivered the opinion of the Court.

School principals in the public school system of the city of Providence, Rhode Island, are permitted to invite members of the clergy to offer invocation and benediction prayers as part of the formal graduation ceremonies for middle schools and for high schools. The question before us is whether including clerical members who offer prayers as part of the official school graduation ceremony is consistent with the Religion Clauses of the First Amendment, provisions the Fourteenth Amendment makes applicable with full force to the States and their school districts.

Deborah Weisman graduated from Nathan Bishop Middle School, a public school in Providence, at a formal ceremony in June 1989. She was about 14 years old. For many years it has been the policy of the Providence School Committee and the Superintendent of Schools to permit principals to invite members of the clergy to give invocations and benedictions at middle school and high school graduations. Many, but not all, of the principals elected to include prayers as part of the graduation ceremonies. Acting for himself and his daughter, Deborah's father, Daniel Weisman, objected to any prayers at Deborah's middle school graduation, but to no avail. The school principal, petitioner Robert E. Lee, invited a rabbi to deliver prayers at the graduation exercises for Deborah's class. Rabbi Leslie Gutterman, of the Temple Beth El in Providence, accepted.

It has been the custom of Providence school officials to provide invited clergy with a pamphlet entitled "Guidelines for Civic Occasions," prepared by the National Conference of Christians and Jews. The Guidelines recommend that public prayers at nonsectarian civic ceremonies be composed with "inclusiveness and sensitivity," though they acknowledge that [p]rayer of any kind may be inappropriate on some civic occasions." App. 20–21. The principal gave Rabbi Gutterman the pamphlet before the graduation and advised him the invocation and benediction should be nonsectarian. Agreed Statement of Facts Par. 17, id., at 13.

Rabbi Gutterman's prayers were as follows:

"INVOCATION

"God of the Free, Hope of the Brave:

"For the legacy of America where diversity is celebrated and the rights of minorities are protected, we thank You. May these young men and women grow up to enrich it.

"For the liberty of America, we thank You. May these new graduates grow up to guard it.

"For the political process of America in which all its citizens may participate, for its court system where all may seek justice we thank You. May those we honor this morning always turn to it in trust.

"For the destiny of America we thank You. May the graduates of Nathan Bishop Middle School so live that they might help to share it.

"May our aspirations for our country and for these young people, who are our hope for the future, be richly fulfilled.

AMEN"

"BENEDICTION

"O God, we are grateful to You for having endowed us with the capacity for learning which we have celebrated on this joyous commencement.

"Happy families give thanks for seeing their children achieve an important milestone. Send Your blessings upon the teachers and administrators who helped prepare them.

"The graduates now need strength and guidance for the future, help them to understand that we are not complete with academic knowledge alone. We must each strive to fulfill what You require of us all: To do justly, to love mercy, to walk humbly.

"We give thanks to You, Lord, for keeping us alive, sustaining us and allowing us to reach this special, happy occasion.

AMEN"

The record in this case is sparse in many respects, and we are unfamiliar with any fixed custom or practice at middle school graduations, referred to by the school district as "promotional exercises." We are not so constrained with reference to high schools, however. High school graduations are such an integral part of American cultural life that we can with confidence describe their customary features, confirmed by aspects of the record and by the parties' representations at oral argument. In the Providence school system, most high school graduation ceremonies are conducted away from the school, while most middle school ceremonies are held on school premises. Classical High School, which Deborah now attends, has conducted its graduation ceremonies on school premises. . . . The parties stipulate that attendance at graduation ceremonies is voluntary. . . . The graduating students enter as a group in a processional, subject to the direction of teachers and school officials, and sit together, apart from their families. We assume the clergy's participation in any high school graduation exercise would be about what it was at Deborah's middle school ceremony. There the students stood for the Pledge of Allegiance and remained standing during the Rabbi's prayers. . . . Even on the assumption that there was a respectful moment of silence both before and after the prayers, the Rabbi's two presentations must not have extended much beyond a minute each, if that. We do not know whether he remained on stage during the whole ceremony, or whether the students received individual diplomas on stage, or if he helped to congratulate them.

The school board (and the United States, which supports it as *amicus curiae*) argued that these short prayers and others like them at graduation exercises are of profound meaning to many students and parents throughout this country who consider that due respect and acknowledgement for divine guidance and for the deepest spiritual aspirations of our people ought to be expressed at an event as important in life as a graduation. We assume this to be so in addressing the difficult case now before us, for the significance of the prayers lies also at the heart of Daniel and Deborah Weisman's case. . . .

The State's role did not end with the decision to include a prayer and with the choice of clergyman. Principal Lee provided Rabbi Gutterman with a copy of the "Guidelines for Civic Occasions," and advised him that his prayers should be nonsectarian. Through these means the principal directed and controlled the content of the prayer. Even if the only sanction for ignoring the instructions were that the rabbi would not be invited back, we think no religious representative who valued his or her continued reputation and effectiveness in the community would incur the State's displeasure in this regard. It is a cornerstone principle of our Establishment Clause jurisprudence that "it is no part of the business of government to compose official prayers for any group of the American people to recite as a part of a religious program carried on by government," *Engel v. Vitale*, 370 U.S. 421, 425 (1962), and that is what the school officials attempted to do. . . .

The First Amendment's Religion Clauses mean that religious beliefs and religious expression are too precious to be either proscribed or prescribed by the State. The design of the Constitution is that preservation and transmission of religious beliefs and worship is a responsibility and a choice committed to the private sphere, which itself is promised freedom to pursue that mission. It must not be forgotten then, that while concern must be given to define the protection granted to an objector or a dissenting nonbeliever, these same Clauses exist to protect religion from government interference. James Madison, the principal author of the Bill of Rights, did not rest his opposition to a religious establishment on the sole ground of its effect on the minority. A principal ground for his view was: "[E]xperience witnesseth that ecclesiastical establishments, instead of maintaining the purity and efficacy of Religion, have had a contrary operation." . . .

Finding no violation under these circumstances would place objectors in the dilemma of participating, with all that implies, or protesting. We do not address whether that choice is acceptable if the affected citizens are mature adults, but we think the State may not, consistent with the Establishment Clause, place primary and secondary school children in this position. Research in psychology supports the common assumption that adolescents are often susceptible to pressure from their peers towards conformity, and that the influence is strongest in matters of social convention. . . .

Our society would be less than true to its heritage if it lacked abiding concern for the values of its young people, and we acknowledge the profound belief of adherents to many faiths that there must be a place in the student's life for precepts of a morality higher even than the law we today enforce. We express no hostility to those aspirations, nor would our oath permit us to do so. A relentless and all-pervasive attempt to exclude religion from every aspect of public life could itself become inconsistent with the Constitution. See *Abington School District, supra*, at 306 (Goldberg, J., concurring). We recognize that, at graduation time and throughout the course of the educational process, there will be instances when religious values, religious practices, and religious persons will have some interaction with the public schools and their students. See *Westside Community Bd. of Ed. v. Mergens*, 496 U.S. 226 (1990). But these matters, often questions of accommodation of religion, are not before us. The sole question presented is whether a religious exercise may be conducted at a graduation ceremony in circumstances where, as we have found, young graduates who object are induced to conform. No holding by this Court suggests that a school can persuade or compel a student to participate in a religious exercise. That is being done here, and it is forbidden by the Establishment Clause of the First Amendment.

For the reasons we have stated, the judgment of the Court of Appeals is *Affirmed.*

Concurring Opinion   JUSTICE BLACKMUN, with whom JUSTICE STEVENS and JUSTICE O'CONNOR join, concurring.

Nearly half a century of review and refinement of Establishment Clause jurisprudence has distilled one clear understanding: Government may neither promote nor affiliate itself with any religious doctrine or organization, nor may it obtrude itself in the internal affairs of any religious institution. The application of these principles to the present case mandates the decision reached today by the Court. . . .

I join the Court's opinion today because I find nothing in it inconsistent with the essential precepts of the Establishment Clause developed in our precedents. The Court holds that the graduation prayer is unconstitutional because the State "in effect required participation in a religious exercise." . . . Although our precedents make clear that proof of government coercion is not necessary to prove an Establishment Clause violation, it is sufficient. Government pressure to participate in a religious activity is an obvious indication that the government is endorsing or promoting religion. . . .

The scope of the Establishment Clause's prohibitions developed in our case law derives from the Clause's purposes. The First Amendment encompasses two distinct guarantees—the government shall make no law respecting an establishment of religion or prohibiting the free exercise . . . thereof—both with the common purpose of securing religious liberty. Through vigorous enforcement of both clauses, we "promote and assure the fullest possible scope of religious liberty and tolerance for all and . . . nurture the conditions which secure the best hope of attainment of that end." *Schempp*, 374 U.S., at 305 (Goldberg, J., concurring). . . .

The mixing of government and religion can be a threat to free government, even if no one is forced to participate. When the government puts its imprimatur on a particular religion, it conveys a message of exclusion to all those who do not adhere to the favored beliefs. A government cannot be premised on the belief that all persons are created equal when it asserts that God prefers some. Only "[a]nguish, hardship and bitter strife" result "when zealous religious groups struggl[e] with one another to obtain the Government's stamp of approval." . . .

It is these understandings and fears that underlie our Establishment Clause jurisprudence. We have believed that religious freedom cannot exist in the absence of a free democratic government, and that such a government cannot endure when there is fusion between religion and the political regime. We have believed that religious freedom cannot thrive in the absence of a vibrant religious community and that such a community cannot prosper when it is bound to the secular. And we have believed that these were the animating principles behind the adoption of the Establishment Clause. To that end, our cases have prohibited government endorsement of religion, its sponsorship, and active involvement in religion, whether or not citizens were coerced to conform.

I remain convinced that our jurisprudence is not misguided, and that it requires the decision reached by the Court today. Accordingly, I join the Court in affirming the judgment of the Court of Appeals.

Concurring Opinion JUSTICE SOUTER, with whom JUSTICE STEVENS and JUSTICE O'CONNOR join, concurring.

I join the whole of the Court's opinion, and fully agree that prayers at public school graduation ceremonies indirectly coerce religious observance. I write separately nonetheless on two issues of Establishment Clause analysis that underlie my independent resolution of this case: whether the Clause applies to governmental practices that do not favor one religion or denomination over others, and whether state coercion of religious conformity, over and above state endorsement of religious exercise or belief, is a necessary element of an Establishment Clause violation.

Forty-five years ago, this Court announced a basic principle of constitutional law from which it has not strayed: the Establishment Clause forbids not only state practices that "aid one religion . . . or prefer one religion over another," but also those that "aid all religions." *Everson v. Board of Education of Ewing*, 330 U.S. 1, 15 (1947). Today we reaffirm that principle, holding that the Establishment Clause forbids state-sponsored prayers in public school settings no matter how nondenominational the prayers may be. In barring the State from sponsoring generically Theistic prayers where it could not sponsor sectarian ones, we hold true to a line of precedent from which there is no adequate historical case to depart.

Since *Everson* we have consistently held the Clause applicable no less to governmental acts favoring religion generally than to acts favoring one religion over others. Thus, in *Engel v. Vitale*, 370 U.S. 421 (1962), we held that the public schools may not subject their students to readings of any prayer, however "denominationally neutral." *Id.*, at 430. More recently, in *Wallace v. Jaffree*, 472 U.S. 38 (1985), we held that an Alabama moment-of-silence statute passed for the sole purpose of "returning voluntary prayer to public schools," *id.*, at 57, violated the Establishment Clause even though it did not encourage students to pray to any particular deity. . . .

When James Madison arrived at the First Congress with a series of proposals to amend the National Constitution, one of the provisions read that "[t]he civil rights of none shall be abridged on account of religious belief or worship, nor shall any national religion be established, nor shall the full and equal rights of conscience be in any manner, or on any pretext, infringed." 1 Annals of Cong. 434 (1789). Madison's language did not last long. It was sent to a Select Committee of the House, which, without explanation, changed it to read that "no religion shall be established by law, nor shall the equal rights of conscience be infringed." *Id.*, at 729. Thence the proposal went to the Committee of the Whole, which was in turn dissatisfied with the Select Committee's language and adopted an alternative proposed by Samuel Livermore of New Hampshire: "Congress shall make no laws touching religion, or infringing the rights of conscience." See *id.*, at 731. Livermore's proposal would have forbidden laws having anything to do with religion and was thus not only far broader than Madison's version, but broader even than the scope of the Establishment Clause as we now understand it. See, *e.g.*, *Corporation of Presiding Bishop of Church of Jesus Christ of Latter-Day Saints v. Amos*, 483 U.S. 327 (1987) (upholding legislative exemption of religious groups from certain obligations under civil rights laws).

The House rewrote the amendment once more before sending it to the Senate, this time adopting, without recorded debate, language derived from a proposal by Fisher Ames of Massachusetts: "Congress shall make no law establishing Religion, or prohibiting the free exercise thereof, nor shall the rights of conscience be infringed." 1 Documentary History of the First Federal Congress of the United States of America 136 (Senate Journal) (L. de Pauw ed. 1972); see 1 Annals of Cong. 765 (1789). Perhaps, on further reflection, the Representatives had thought Livermore's proposal too expansive, or perhaps, as one historian has suggested, they had simply worried that his language would not "satisfy the demands of those who wanted something said specifically against establishments of religion." L. Levy, The Establishment Clause 81 (1986) (hereinafter Levy). We do not know; what we do know is that the House rejected the Select Committee's version, which arguably ensured only that "no religion" enjoyed an official preference over others, and deliberately chose instead a prohibition extending to laws establishing "religion" in general.

The sequence of the Senate's treatment of this House proposal, and the House's response to the Senate, confirm that the Framers meant the Establishment Clause's prohibition to encompass nonpreferential aid to religion. In September 1789, the Senate considered a number of provisions that would have permitted such aid, and ultimately it adopted one of them. First, it briefly entertained this language: "Congress shall make no law establishing One Religious Sect or Society in preference to others, nor shall the rights of conscience be infringed." 1 Documentary History, *supra*, at 151 (Senate Journal). After rejecting two minor amendments to that proposal, see*ibid.*, the Senate dropped it altogether and chose a provision identical to the House's proposal, but without the clause protecting the "rights of conscience," *ibid.* With no record of the Senate debates, we cannot know what prompted these changes, but the record does tell us that, six days later, the Senate went half circle and adopted its narrowest language yet: "Congress shall make no law establishing articles of faith or a mode of worship, or prohibiting the free exercise of religion." *Id.*, at 166. The Senate sent this proposal to the House along with its versions of the other constitutional amendments proposed.

Though it accepted much of the Senate's work on the Bill of Rights, the House rejected the Senate's version of the Establishment Clause and called for a joint conference committee, to which the Senate agreed. The House conferees ultimately won out, persuading the Senate to accept this as the final text of the Religion Clauses: "Congress shall make no law respecting an establishment of religion, or prohibiting the free exercise thereof." What is remarkable is that, unlike the earliest House drafts or the final Senate proposal, the prevailing language is not limited to laws respecting an establishment of "a religion," "a national religion," "one religious sect," or specific "articles of faith." The Framers repeatedly considered and deliberately rejected such narrow language and instead extended their prohibition to state support for "religion" in general. . . .

Religious students cannot complain that omitting prayers from their graduation ceremony would, in any realistic sense, "burden" their spiritual callings. To be sure, many of them invest this rite of passage with spiritual significance, but they may express their religious feelings about it before and after the ceremony. They may even organize a privately sponsored baccalaureate if they desire the company of like-minded students. Because they accordingly have no need for the machinery of the State to affirm their beliefs, the government's sponsorship of prayer at the graduation ceremony is most reasonably understood as an official endorsement of religion and, in this instance, of Theistic religion. . . .

When public school officials, armed with the State's authority, convey an endorsement of religion to their students, they strike near the core of the Establishment Clause. However "ceremonial" their messages may be, they are flatly unconstitutional.

Dissenting Opinion   JUSTICE SCALIA, with whom THE CHIEF JUSTICE, JUSTICE WHITE, and JUSTICE THOMAS join, dissenting.

Three Terms ago, I joined an opinion recognizing that the Establishment Clause must be construed in light of the "[g]overnment policies of accommodation, acknowledgment, and support for religion [that] are an accepted part of our political and cultural heritage." That opinion affirmed that "the meaning of the Clause is to be determined by reference to historical practices and understandings." It said that "[a] test for implementing the protections of the Establishment Clause that, if applied with consistency, would invalidate longstanding traditions cannot be a proper reading of the Clause." *Allegheny County v. Greater Pittsburgh ACLU*, 492 U.S. 573, 657, 670 (1989) (Kennedy, J., concurring in judgment in part and dissenting in part).

These views of course prevent me from joining today's opinion, which is conspicuously bereft of any reference to history. In holding that the Establishment Clause prohibits invocations and benedictions at public-school graduation ceremonies, the Court—with nary a mention that it is doing so—lays waste a tradition that is as old as public-school graduation ceremonies themselves, and that is a component of an even more longstanding American tradition of nonsectarian prayer to God at public celebrations generally. As its instrument of destruction, the bulldozer of its social engineering, the Court invents a boundless, and boundlessly manipulable, test of psychological coercion, which promises to do for the Establishment Clause what the *Durham* rule did for the insanity defense. See *Durham v. United States*, 94 U.S.App.D.C. 228, 214 F.2d 862 (1954). Today's opinion shows more forcefully than volumes of argumentation why our Nation's protection, that fortress which is our Constitution, cannot possibly rest upon the changeable philosophical predilections of the Justices of this Court, but must have deep foundations in the historic practices of our people. . . .

From our Nation's origin, prayer has been a prominent part of governmental ceremonies and proclamations. The Declaration of Independence, the document marking our birth as a separate people, "appeal[ed] to the Supreme Judge of the world for the rectitude of our intentions" and avowed "a firm reliance on the protection of divine Providence." In his first inaugural address, after swearing his oath of office on a Bible, George Washington deliberately made a prayer a part of his first official act as President. . . .

In addition to this general tradition of prayer at public ceremonies, there exists a more specific tradition of invocations and benedictions at public-school graduation exercises. . . .

The Court presumably would separate graduation invocations and benedictions from other instances of public "preservation and transmission of religious beliefs" on the ground that they involve "psychological coercion." I find it a sufficient embarassment that our Establishment Clause jurisprudence regarding holiday displays, see *Allegheny County v. Greater Pittsburgh ACLU*, 492 U.S. 573 (1989), has come to "requir[e] scrutiny more commonly associated with interior decorators than with the judiciary." *American Jewish Congress v. Chicago*, 827 F.2d 120, 129 (Easterbrook, J., dissenting). But interior decorating is a rock-hard science compared to psychology practiced by amateurs. A few citations of "[r]esearch in psychology" that have no particular bearing upon the precise issue here . . . cannot disguise the fact that the Court has gone beyond the realm where judges know what they are doing. The Court's argument that state officials have "coerced" students to take part in the invocation and benediction at graduation ceremonies is, not to put too fine a point on it, incoherent. . . .

The narrow context of the present case involves a community's celebration of one of the milestones in its young citizens' lives, and it is a bold step for this Court to seek to banish from that occasion, and from thousands of similar celebrations throughout this land, the expression of gratitude to God that a majority of the community wishes to make. The issue before us today is not the abstract philosophical question whether the alternative of frustrating this desire of a religious majority is to be preferred over the alternative of imposing "psychological coercion," or a feeling of exclusion, upon nonbelievers. Rather, the question is *whether a mandatory choice in favor of the former has been imposed by the United States Constitution*. As the age-old practices of our people show, the answer to that question is not at all in doubt.

I must add one final observation: The founders of our Republic knew the fearsome potential of sectarian religious belief to generate civil dissension and civil strife. And they also knew that nothing, absolutely nothing, is so inclined to foster among religious believers of various faiths a toleration—no, an affection—for one another than voluntarily joining in prayer together, to the God whom they all worship and seek. Needless to say, no one should be compelled to do that, but it is a shame to deprive our public culture of the opportunity, and indeed the encouragement, for people to do it voluntarily. The Baptist or Catholic who heard and joined in the simple and inspiring prayers of Rabbi Gutterman on this official and patriotic occasion was inoculated from religious bigotry and prejudice in a manner that can not be replicated. To deprive our society of that important unifying mechanism, in order to spare the nonbeliever what seems to me the minimal inconvenience of standing or even sitting in respectful nonparticipation, is as senseless in policy as it is unsupported in law.

For the foregoing reasons, I dissent.

·······················DISCUSSION QUESTIONS ·······················

1. How much weight should today's justices give to what the authors of the Constitution intended two centuries ago?
2. What advice would you give to a state legislature that wanted to write a law requiring a moment of silence in public schools?
3. How difficult do you think it would be for a student to leave the classroom while the teacher was reciting a prayer?
4. Would it be acceptable to read Bible verses over a school's public-address system if the teachings of other religions were also read from time to time?
5. Would it be acceptable to post the Ten Commandments in public school classrooms if similar lists from other religions were also posted?
6. Do you think that there is a fundamental difference between a prayer recited in a schoolroom and a prayer recited in front of a state legislature? How are they similar? How are they different? Do you agree that the members of a legislature are less likely to pay attention to an official prayer than are schoolchildren?
7. In your opinion, does the requirement that creation-science be given equal teaching time with the theory of evolution advance religion?
8. Could a prayer be written for use in a public school that did not violate the Establishment Clause? If so, what would it say?

CHAPTER
three

• • • • • • • • •

Government Support for Religious Schools

•••••••••••••••••••••••••••••••••• DISCUSSION ••••••••••••••••••••••••••••••••••

The Establishment Clause of the First Amendment states that Congress cannot "establish" a religion. For the first century and a half of the United States' existence, Congress did very little that could be considered "establishing" religion; the issue simply did not come up much. By the end of the 1930s, however, the U.S. Supreme Court had determined that the Fourteenth Amendment made the First Amendment of the U.S. Constitution applicable to state and local governments as well as the federal government. The issue of "establishing" religion was raised more frequently with regard to the actions of state and local governments. How would the New Deal Court deal with this issue? In 1947 the Court began to provide an answer to that question.

GOVERNMENT REIMBURSEMENT OF BUS FARE

The case, *Everson v. Board of Education* (see p. 44), involved a New Jersey law that stated that parents who sent their children to public or Catholic school could receive a reimbursement from the state for any money spent on bus fare. While many of the Catholic schools had scholarships to help poor children attend, some parents lived far from the nearest Catholic school and could not afford to pay the bus fare. The state reasoned that every child that attended Catholic school was one less child the state had to pay to educate, and it would be less expensive for the state to pay the bus fare than to build the dozens of new public schools that would be needed if those children could not attend Catholic school. Some New Jersey taxpayers objected that this practice, at least to the extent that it provided funds to children attending Catholic school, amounted to an "establishment" of religion and so violated the First Amendment. The Court divided five to four in coming to a decision.

Justice Black, writing for the five-justice majority, held that this New Jersey practice was not a violation of the First Amendment and did not amount to "establishing" a religion. Most of the people who voted to place the First Amendment in the Constitution, Justice Black noted, had lived under an established church in the days before the American Revolution. In Justice Black's opinion, what these people had in mind when they voted to prevent future generations from establishing a religion probably had nothing to do with paying bus fare for little children on their way to school, but instead with such things as using tax dollars to build churches or to pay ministers to preach only the accepted religious doctrine.

Justice Black summarized what he believed the Establishment Clause meant by saying:

> The "establishment of religion" clause of the First Amendment means at least this: Neither a state nor the Federal Government can set up a church. Neither can pass laws which aid one religion, aid all religions, or prefer one religion over another. Neither can force nor influence a person to go to or to remain away from church against his will or force him to profess a belief or disbelief in any religion. No person can be punished for entertaining or professing religious beliefs or disbeliefs, for church attendance or nonattendance. No tax in any amount, large or small, can be levied to support any religious activities or institutions, whatever they may be called, or whatever form they may adopt to teach or practice religion. Neither a state nor the Federal Government can, openly or secretly, participate in the affairs of any religious organizations or groups or vice versa. In the words of Jefferson, the clause against establishment of religion by law was intended to erect "a wall of separation between church and state."

He did not see any similarities between providing parents with funds to reimburse them for the cost of transporting their children to Catholic school and using tax dollars to build churches or to pay ministers.

The majority of the Supreme Court was also mindful of the financial reality of the case. If all of the children who attended Catholic school in New Jersey suddenly began to attend public school instead, then the public school system would be overwhelmed. The children were receiving an education at little or no cost to the taxpayers. In fact, it could be argued that while this group of New Jersey taxpayers objected to having their tax dollars pay for transporting children to Catholic school, they were really getting a bargain compared with the cost of educating those same children in public school.

The majority of justices thought that all the state was doing was paying to transport children to school. Surely a state could provide free transportation to children without regard to their destination. If the state provided free transportation to everyone *except* people going to Catholic school, wouldn't this violate the First Amendment provision that forbids interference with the "free exercise" of religion?

Four justices dissented. They pointed out that the state of New Jersey was not exactly providing free transportation to all children regardless of where they wanted to go. If the state had been, then there would have been no objection. Instead, the state of New Jersey was providing free transportation only to children attending public school or Catholic school. Children going anywhere else, including other private schools, did not receive free transportation. The dissenting justices argued that if the state sent a check directly to the Catholic schools to pay for buses, this would clearly violate the Establishment Clause; the fact that the money was sent to the parents instead of the schools should not be the deciding factor.

The main issue of the case was: What should be the deciding factor? The dissenting justices believed that the state was spending money to help parents send their children to a school where they received religious indoctrination. If the state could not give this support directly, by providing the buses itself or by paying the Catholic schools to provide the buses, then it should not be allowed to do the same thing indirectly by paying money to the parents.

Justice Jackson, in his dissenting opinion, argued that it would clearly be illegal for the state to provide free transportation only to people going to Catholic church. While he would allow the state to provide free transportation to all children regardless of their destination, in his opinion providing free transportation only to Roman Catholic children on their way to Roman Catholic school was unconstitutional.

Justice Rutledge, in his dissenting opinion, stated that the wall of separation that Thomas Jefferson had spoken of should be high and should forbid "every form of public aid or support for religion," including helping children attend Catholic school.

RELIGIOUS INSTRUCTION IN PUBLIC SCHOOLS

The next year, in McCollum v. Board of Education, the Court came to a unanimous conclusion. The case involved the Champaign Illinois Board of Education's practice of allowing religious teachers to come into the public schools once a week to provide religious instruction. There was no cost to the taxpayers other than the use of public school property, but the justices thought that the use of public school property was exactly what made this practice illegal.

While in *Everson v. Board of Education* the Court had ruled that providing some indirect support to children attending private religious schools was permissible, in *McCollum v. Board of Education* the Court decided that allowing religious indoctrination to take place on public school grounds clearly amounted to government support for a particular religion or group of religions and was not permissible. While attendance was voluntary for the children, the justices believed that the children would be pressured to attend the religion classes.

"RELEASE TIME" FOR RELIGIOUS INSTRUCTION

A few years later, a majority of justices agreed that a state could allow students attending public school to be "released" to receive religious instruction away from the public school (*Zorach v. Clausen*). This "release time" policy avoided excessive entanglement between school and church. Children could attend any church they chose, and those who did not attend would remain at public school. Because no public funds or public buildings were used, the justices thought that there was less of a chance that people might see this as government support for religion. Six of the justices believed that this practice was more in the nature of an "accommodation" with religion rather than "support" for religion. Of course drawing the line between accommodation and support is not easy.

Justices Black, Frankfurter, and Jackson each wrote their own dissenting opinions. The dissenting justices believed that there was an important distinction between students' attending religious classes after the close of the regular school day and allowing students to leave public school early only if they went straight to religious instruction. The former would certainly be permissible. The latter amounted to encouraging students to attend religious instruction, and therefore, in the opinion of the dissenting justices, violated the First Amendment. Justice Black thought that the sole question was whether New York could "use its compulsory education laws to help religious sects get attendants presumably too unenthusiastic to go unless moved to do so by the pressure of this state machinery." He believed that the obvious answer to this question was no.

TEXTBOOK LENDING TO PRIVATE SCHOOLS

It would be 1968 before the Court would again face the issue of government support for religious schools. The case, *Board of Education v. Allen* (see p. 51), involved a New York statute that required public schools to lend textbooks to children attending private schools, including religious private schools. Six of the nine justices thought that this was perfectly legal. After all, wasn't this similar to the New Jersey practice of reimbursing parents for bus fare, which the

Court had allowed two decades before in *Everson v. Board of Education*? In that case it was acceptable for a state to provide free transportation to children, so in this case it should be acceptable for a state to provide free books to children. It had not mattered in the *Everson* case that the children were riding the free transportation to Catholic school. In the *Allen* case it should not matter that the children were taking the textbooks to private religious schools, or even that the loaned textbooks would probably be passed out at those schools.

One of the interesting things about the *Allen* case is that two of the three justices who wrote dissenting opinions in *Allen* had voted with the majority in *Everson*. Justices Black and Douglas used their dissenting opinions to argue that there is a very important distinction between providing free bus transportation to children going to Catholic school and providing free textbooks to children who attend private religious schools. Justice Black called the practice of lending textbooks to children in religious schools a "flat, flagrant, open violation" of the First Amendment. It was difficult for the other justices to see the difference.

THE *LEMON* TEST

In 1971 the Court handed down two decisions that would be used as a guide for many years after. The first case, *Lemon v. Kurtzman*, involved the practice in Rhode Island and Pennsylvania of providing a supplement to the salary of Catholic schoolteachers. Again, the reason for doing this was that it was much less expensive for the state governments to give some financial support to Catholic schools than to have to provide public education for all of the Catholic school students if those schools closed.

Eight members of the Court found this salary supplement to be a clearly unconstitutional attempt to "establish" religion. Paying money directly to religious schools was direct government support of religion. While *Everson* and *Allen* allowed governments to provide some indirect support to religious schools, in *Lemon* governments were actually paying money to private religious schools to help pay teachers' salaries. Only Justice White dissented from this opinion.

The second case, *Tilton v. Richardson*, involved the federal Higher Education Facilities Act, which provided funds to colleges, both public and private, to build buildings, in the face of an exploding college-age population. Some of the colleges that would receive support under the act were affiliated with religions. With a vote of five to four, the Court ruled that this act was constitutional.

Developing the *Lemon* Test

In drawing the distinction between providing salary supplements to religious high schools (unconstitutional) and providing funds to build buildings on religious college campuses (constitutional), the Court developed what has come to be called the "*Lemon* test." The test gives four steps for determining whether a law violates the First Amendment. The court will examine the law to see whether it: (1) has a secular purpose; (2) has a primary effect of advancing or inhibiting religion; (3) fosters excessive government entanglement with religion; and (4) inhibits the free exercise of religion.

The Court believed that a government practice of regularly providing money to religious schools below the college level for salary supplements violated the *Lemon* test because it would advance religion and foster excessive entanglement between government and religion. On the other hand, a majority of the justices thought that paying to build a few buildings on college campuses, buildings that would not be used for religious indoctrination, would not advance religion or foster excessive entanglement. By excessive entanglement the Court meant too much government interference with the daily operations of a religion.

While the Court talked about entanglement, there was another important factor. The money in the *Tilton* case was going to colleges. The money in the *Lemon* case was going to support religious education below the college level. In the opinion of the Court, college students are less susceptible to religious indoctrination, and very little religious indoctrination actually goes on in college, even in those colleges nominally affiliated with a particular religion. On the other hand, one of the primary funtions of most religious schools below the college level is to provide extensive religious indoctrination.

Applying the *Lemon* Test

In two 1973 cases, the Court came to the same conclusions. Governments could not spend large sums of money to reimburse religious schools for a variety of costs, but governments could provide funds to colleges, even religious colleges, to build buildings (*Levitt v. Public Education*, *Hunt v. McNair*).

Also in 1973 the Court ruled that states could not reimburse parents, either through direct payments or through the use of a tax credit, for the cost of tuition spent to send children to religious schools (*Committee v. Nyquist*, *Sloan v. Lemon*). A majority of the justices believed that this support for religious schools was too direct. If government could not pay directly to supplement salaries of teachers at religious schools, then it could not reimburse parents for the cost of tuition.

In 1975 the Court ruled that while a state could lend textbooks to private religious schools, it could not lend other teaching materials or equipment, because this would result in excessive entanglement between government and religion and would violate the *Lemon* test (*Meek v. Pittenger*).

In 1976 the Court ruled, five to four, that the state of Maryland could provide grants to private colleges, even those colleges affiliated with a religion (*Roemer v. Board of Public Works*). While these were nominally religious colleges, they provided a basically secular education with little religious indoctrination. The Court majority believed that the grants would serve the secular purpose of relieving some of the pressure on the state colleges, and that, because the schools in question were colleges, there was less chance that the grants would be seen as a government endorsement of religion.

In 1980, in *Committee for Public Education v. Regan*, the Court ruled five to four that the state of New York could reimburse private religious schools for the cost of giving standard tests that the state required be given to all schoolchildren. A majority of the justices thought that this reimbursement would not foster too much entanglement between the government and the schools and would not have the primary effect of advancing religion.

In 1983 five justices decided that Minnesota could allow state taxpayers to deduct from their income for state income-tax purposes the expense of paying for "tuition, textbooks and transportation" so their children could attend private schools, even private religious schools (*Mueller v. Allen*). The Court had to decide whether tax deductions were more like bus fare reimbursements and loaned textbooks, which were allowed in *Everson* and *Board of Education v. Allen*, or more like direct subsidies and tuition reimbursements, which were ruled unconstitutional in *Nyquist* and *Sloan*. A majority of the justices believed that this tax deduction was more like the indirect support of *Everson* and *Allen* than the direct subsidy of *Nyquist* and *Sloan*.

The majority applied the *Lemon* test and found that the tax deduction had a secular purpose—to advance education; had a primary effect that did not advance religion; and would not cause much entanglement between religion and government. Because the state allowed all parents to deduct all educational expenses, even those related to sending their children to public school, the Court thought that it was reasonable for the state to allow the deduction for private school expenses as well. The key distinction in this case was between direct support to private religious schools below the college level, which is not permissible, and indirect support, which is.

The four dissenting justices believed that this was simply a case of the state doing indirectly what it could not do directly. They argued that the former cases that allowed for some indirect support had been wrongly decided, in part because they led to this result.

Justice Powell was the swing vote in both *Nyquist* and *Mueller*. In *Nyquist* the state wanted to provide a tax credit, which he thought was too direct a support for religious schools. In *Mueller* he held that a tax deduction was acceptable. What is the difference between a tax credit and a tax deduction? With a tax credit, taxpayers figure out how much income tax they owe and then subtract the amount of the tax credit from their tax bill. For example, if the tax credit is $500 and the taxpayer would have owed $1,000 in taxes, then with the tax credit, he or she now only owes $500. A tax deduction, on the other hand, is an amount that is subtracted from the taxable income. If the tax deduction is $2,000 and the taxpayer would otherwise have a taxable income of $20,000, then after the deduction, he or she would have a taxable income of only $18,000.

A tax credit can be seen as very similar to a direct payment from the state. Instead of sending out a check for $500, the state simply tells taxpayers to keep $500 when paying their tax bills. A tax deduction is much less like a direct government subsidy. A tax deduction says that if part of a person's income is used for certain purposes, among them sending a child to school, then that part will not be subject to income tax.

In 1985 the Court split five to four the other way. This case, *Aguilar v. Felton*, involved the practice in New York City of sending public school teachers to private religious schools to provide remedial education and counseling. Because this practice required sending government employees to work in private religious schools, a majority of the justices thought that it involved too much entanglement between government and religion.

CONCLUSION

Throughout the half century that the Supreme Court has been trying to determine what is constitutional government support for private religious schools and what is unconstitutional support, there have been those who have called for a simple test that would outlaw any kind of support, direct or indirect, for religious schools, regardless of the level of instruction. A very high wall between church and state would be easy to see and would provide a simple guide.

In the 1960s Justice Douglas regretted that back in 1947, in the *Everson* case, he had not voted to begin constructing such a high wall. When he voted in *Everson*, he had not expected that all of these situations would come up, or that the Court would face so many problems in trying to draw meaningful distinctions between what is constitutional in this area and what is unconstitutional.

Justice Clark's warning in *Schempp* (the Bible readings in public schools case) that what is a "trickling stream" today may become a "raging torrent" tomorrow certainly seems to have come true. The fact remains that in the *Everson* case Justice Douglas did vote to allow New Jersey to reimburse parents for the cost of transporting their children to Catholic school.

Throughout the decades that followed that decision, a majority of justices have held that governments can provide some indirect support for religious schools below the college level and some direct support for religious colleges without violating the First Amendment's Establishment Clause. In handing down these decisions, the justices have developed a number of important distinctions. They have accepted the idea that money provided to colleges would be seen more as government support for higher education than as support for religion. Because most private colleges in the United States are at least nominally affiliated with a religion, to rule otherwise would have prevented most government support to most private colleges. At the same time, the justices believed that because religious schools below the college level engage in religious indoctrination to an extensive degree, "direct" support for these schools would constitute "establishing" religion, but some indirect support would be permissible. In trying to draw the line between direct support and indirect support, the Court outlawed most direct payments to such schools and tuition reimbursement, but allowed bus fare reimbursements and the lending of textbooks. The Court believed an important distinction could be drawn between tuition reimbursements and tax credits on the one hand, which amounted to using government tax money to support religion, and tax deductions on the other.

Throughout the last half of the twentieth century, the justices have become more and more sensitive to the need to treat all religions, and atheism, equally. In 1947, in the *Everson* case, the justices spent little time discussing the fact that only one group of religious schools, Roman Catholic, qualified for bus fare reimbursement. In the 1990s this would have been a major focus of the Court and a reason to declare the law unconstitutional.

Over the years the Court has been forced to recognize that in the area of government support for religious schools, the prohibition against establishing religion comes into conflict with the prohibition against interfering with religious freedom. The Court has said on many occasions that parents have the right to send their children to religious schools. If those schools close, that right will be meaningless.

Different religious groups have held different opinions about government financial support for religious schools. Those religious sects that make a significant effort to provide private education for their children have argued for increased government support for private religious schools. Those sects that do not emphasize private education for their children have not favored government support of private religious education.

While some justices, such as Justice Douglas, have wished that they could turn back the hands of time and vote differently, that is not possible. The wall of separation between government and religious schools is not absolute. It is low as far as religious colleges are concerned, and higher for schools under the college level.

CASE DECISIONS

Everson v. Board of Education and *Board of Education v. Allen* are concerned with the extent to which government may provide financial support for religious schools below the college level. Justice Black wrote the majority decision in *Everson v. Board of Education*. Four justices dissented, and Justices Jackson and Rutledge wrote dissenting opinions, which are also included here. This decision held that the state of New Jersey could reimburse parents for the cost of transporting their children to Catholic schools.

Two decades later, with the case of *Board of Education v. Allen*, the Court faced the question of whether or not the state of New York could supply free textbooks to religious schools. Justice White wrote the opinion for the six-justice majority, holding that this practice was constitutional. Justice Harlan wrote a concurring opinion, which is included here. Three justices dissented, and Justices Black and Douglas wrote dissenting opinions, which are also included here. Their dissenting opinions are of particular interest because they voted with the majority in the *Everson* case.

Following are excerpts from the case decisions.

* * * * * * * * * *

EVERSON v. BOARD OF EDUCATION
330 U.S. 1 (1947)

MR. JUSTICE BLACK delivered the opinion of the Court.

A New Jersey statute authorizes its local school districts to make rules and contracts for the transportation of children to and from schools. The appellee, a township board of education, acting pursuant to this statute, authorized reimbursement to parents of money expended by them for the bus transportation of their children on regular busses operated by the public transportation system. Part of this money was for the payment of transportation of some children in the community to Catholic parochial schools. These church schools give their students, in addition to secular education, regular religious instruction conforming to the religious tenets and modes of worship of the Catholic Faith. The superintendent of these schools is a Catholic priest. . . .

The New Jersey statute is challenged as a "law respecting an establishment of religion." The First Amendment, as made applicable to the states by the Fourteenth, *Murdock v. Pennsylvania*, 319 U.S. 105, commands that a state "shall make no law respecting an establishment of religion, or prohibiting the free exercise thereof . . . ." These words of the First Amendment reflected in the minds of early Americans a vivid mental picture of conditions and practices which they fervently wished to stamp out in order to preserve liberty for themselves and for their posterity. Doubtless their goal has not been entirely reached; but so far has the Nation moved toward it that the expression "law respecting an establishment of religion," probably does not so vividly remind present-day Americans of the evils, fears, and political problems that caused that expression to be written into our Bill of Rights. Whether this New Jersey law is one respecting an "establishment of religion" requires an understanding of the meaning of that language, particularly with respect to the imposition of taxes. Once again, therefore, it is not inappropriate briefly to review the background and environment of the period in which that constitutional language was fashioned and adopted.

A large proportion of the early settlers of this country came here from Europe to escape the bondage of laws which compelled them to support and attend government-favored churches. The centuries immediately before and contemporaneous with the colonization of America had been filled with turmoil, civil strife, and persecutions, generated in large part by established sects determined to maintain their absolute political and religious supremacy. With the power of government supporting them, at various times and places, Catholics had persecuted Protestants, Protestants had persecuted Catholics, Protestant sects had persecuted other Protestant sects, Catholics of one shade of belief had persecuted Catholics of another shade of belief, and all of these had from time to time persecuted Jews. In efforts to force loyalty to whatever religious group happened to be on top and in league with the government of a particular time and place, men and women had been fined, cast in jail, cruelly tortured, and killed. Among the offenses for which these punishments had been inflicted were such things as speaking disrespectfully of the views of ministers of government-established churches, non-attendance at those churches, expressions of non-belief in their doctrines, and failure to pay taxes and tithes to support them. . . .

These practices became so commonplace as to shock the freedom-loving colonials into a feeling of abhorrence. The imposition of taxes to pay ministers' salaries and to build and maintain churches and church property aroused their indignation. It was these feelings which found expression in the First Amendment. No one locality and no one group throughout the Colonies can rightly be given entire credit for having aroused the sentiment that culminated in adoption of the Bill of Rights' provisions embracing religious liberty. But Virginia, where the established church had achieved a dominant influence in political affairs and where many excesses attracted wide public attention, provided a great stimulus and able leadership for the movement. The people there, as elsewhere, reached the conviction that individual religious liberty could be achieved best under a government which was stripped of all power to tax, to support, or otherwise to assist any or all religions, or to interfere with the beliefs of any religious individual or group. . . .

The "establishment of religion" clause of the First Amendment means at least this: Neither a state nor the Federal Government can set up a church. Neither can pass laws which aid one religion, aid all religions, or prefer one religion over another. Neither can force nor influence a person to go to or to remain away from church against his will or force him to profess a belief or disbelief in any religion. No person can be punished for entertaining or professing religious beliefs or disbeliefs, for church attendance or non-attendance. No tax in any amount, large or small, can be levied to support any religious activities or institutions, whatever they may be called, or whatever form they may adopt to teach or practice religion. Neither a state nor the Federal Government can, openly or secretly, participate in the affairs of any religious organizations or groups and *vice versa*. In the words of Jefferson, the clause against establishment of religion by law was intended to erect "a wall of separation between church and State." *Reynolds v. United States, supra* at 164.

We must consider the New Jersey statute in accordance with the foregoing limitations imposed by the First Amendment. But we must not strike that state statute down if it is within the State's constitutional power even though it approaches the verge of that power. See *Interstate Ry. v. Massachusetts*, Holmes, J., *supra* 85, 88. New Jersey cannot consistently with the "establishment of religion" clause of the First Amendment contribute tax-raised funds to the support of an institution which teaches the tenets and faith of any church. On the other hand, other language of the amendment commands that New Jersey cannot hamper its citizens in the free exercise of their own religion. Consequently, it cannot exclude individual Catholics, Lutherans, Mohammedans, Baptists, Jews, Methodists, Non-believers, Presbyterians, or the members of any other faith, *because of their faith, or lack of it*, from receiving the benefits of public welfare legislation. While we do not mean to intimate that a state could not provide transportation only to children attending public schools, we must be careful, in protecting the citizens of New Jersey against state-established churches, to be sure that we do not inadvertently prohibit New Jersey from extending its general state law benefits to all its citizens without regard to their religious belief.

Measured by these standards, we cannot say that the First Amendment prohibits New Jersey from spending tax-raised funds to pay the bus fares of parochial school pupils as a part of a general program under which it pays the fares of pupils attending public and other schools. It is undoubtedly true that children are helped to get to church schools. There is even a possibility that some of the children might not be sent to the church schools if the parents were compelled to pay their children's bus fares out of their own pockets when transportation to a public school would have been paid for by the State. The same possibility exists where the state requires a local transit company to provide reduced fares to school children including those attending parochial schools, or where a municipally owned transportation system undertakes to carry all school children free of charge. Moreover, state-paid policemen, detailed to protect children going to and from church schools from the very real hazards of traffic, would serve much the same purpose and accomplish much the same result as state provisions intended to guarantee free transportation of a kind which the state deems to be best for the school children's welfare. And parents might refuse to risk their children to the serious danger of traffic accidents going to and from parochial schools, the approaches to which were not protected by policemen. Similarly, parents might be reluctant to permit their children to attend schools which the state had cut off from such general government services as ordinary police and fire protection, connections for sewage disposal, public highways and sidewalks. Of course, cutting off church schools from these services, so separate and so indisputably marked off from the religious function, would make it far more difficult for the schools to operate. But such is obviously not the purpose of the First Amendment. That Amendment requires the state to be a neutral in its relations with groups of religious believers and non-believers; it does not require the state to be their adversary. State power is no more to be used so as to handicap religions than it is to favor them.

This Court has said that parents may, in the discharge of their duty under state compulsory education laws, send their children to a religious rather than a public school if the school meets the secular educational requirements which the state has power to impose. See *Pierce v. Society of Sisters*, 268 U.S. 510. It appears that these parochial schools meet New Jersey's requirements. The State contributes no money to the schools. It does not support them. Its legislation, as applied, does no more than provide a general program to help parents get their children, regardless of their religion, safely and expeditiously to and from accredited schools.

The First Amendment has erected a wall between church and state. That wall must be kept high and impregnable. We could not approve the slightest breach. New Jersey has not breached it here.

Affirmed.

Dissenting Opinion   MR. JUSTICE JACKSON, dissenting.

I find myself, contrary to first impressions, unable to join in this decision. I have a sympathy, though it is not ideological, with Catholic citizens who are compelled by law to pay taxes for public schools, and also feel constrained by conscience and discipline to support other schools for their own children. Such relief to them as this case involves is not in itself a serious burden to taxpayers and I had assumed it to be as little serious in principle. Study of this case convinces me otherwise. The Court's opinion marshals every argument in favor of state aid and puts the case in its most favorable light, but much of its reasoning confirms my conclusions that there are not good grounds upon which to support the present legislation. In fact, the undertones of the opinion, advocating complete and uncompromising separation of Church from State, seem utterly discordant with its conclusion yielding support to their commingling in educational matters. The case which irresistibly comes to mind as the most fitting precedent is that of Julia who, according to Byron's reports, "whispering 'I will ne'er consent,'—consented."

The Court sustains this legislation by assuming two deviations from the facts of this particular case; first, it assumes a state of facts the record does not support, and secondly, it refuses to consider facts which are inescapable on the record.

The Court concludes that this "legislation, as applied, does no more than provide a general program to help parents get their children, regardless of their religion, safely and expeditiously to and from accredited schools," and it draws a comparison between "state provisions intended to guarantee free transportation" for school children with services such as police and fire protection, and implies that we are here dealing with "laws authorizing new types of public services . . ." This hypothesis permeates the opinion. The facts will not bear that construction.

The Township of Ewing is not furnishing transportation to the children in any form; it is not operating school busses itself or contracting for their operation; and it is not performing any public service of any kind with this taxpayer's money. All school children are left to ride as ordinary paying passengers on the regular busses operated by the public transportation system. What the Township does, and what the taxpayer complains of, is at stated intervals to reimburse parents for the fares paid, provided the children attend either public schools or Catholic Church schools. This expenditure of tax funds has no possible effect on the child's safety or expedition in transit. As passengers on the public busses they travel as fast and no faster, and are as safe and no safer, since their parents are reimbursed as before.

In addition to thus assuming a type of service that does not exist, the Court also insists that we must close our eyes to a discrimination which does exist. The resolution which authorizes disbursement of this taxpayer's money limits reimbursement to those who attend public schools and Catholic schools. That is the way the Act is applied to this taxpayer.

The New Jersey Act in question makes the character of the school, not the needs of the children, determine the eligibility of parents to reimbursement. The Act permits payment for transportation to parochial schools or public schools but prohibits it to private schools operated in whole or in part for profit. Children often are sent to private schools because their parents feel that they require more individual instruction than public schools can provide, or because they are backward or defective and need special attention. If all children of the state were objects of impartial solicitude, no reason is obvious for denying transportation reimbursement to students of this class, for these often are as needy and as worthy as those who go to public or parochial schools. Refusal to reimburse those who attend such schools is understandable only in the light of a purpose to aid the schools, because the state might well abstain from aiding a profit-making private enterprise. Thus, under the Act and resolution brought to us by this case, children are classified according to the schools they attend and are to be aided if they attend the public schools or private Catholic schools, and they are not allowed to be aided if they attend private secular schools or private religious schools of other faiths. . . .

The Court's holding is that this taxpayer has no grievance because the state has decided to make the reimbursement a public purpose and therefore we are bound to regard it as such. I agree that this Court has left, and always should leave to each state, great latitude in deciding for itself, in the light of its own conditions, what shall be public purposes in its scheme of things. It may socialize utilities and economic enterprises and make taxpayers' business out of what conventionally had been private business. It may make public business of individual welfare, health, education, entertainment or security. But it cannot make public business of religious worship or instruction, or of attendance at religious institutions of any character. There is no answer to the proposition, more fully expounded by Mr. Justice Rutledge, that the effect of the religious freedom Amendment to our Constitution was to take every form of propagation of religion out of the realm of things which could directly or indirectly be made public business and thereby be supported in whole or in part at taxpayers' expense. That is a difference which the Constitution sets up between religion and almost every other subject matter of legislation, a difference which goes to the very root of religious freedom and which the Court is overlooking today. This freedom was first in the Bill of Rights because it was first in the forefathers' minds; it was set forth in absolute terms, and its strength is its rigidity. It was intended not only to keep the states' hands out of religion, but to keep religion's hands off the state, and, above all, to keep bitter religious controversy out of public life by denying to every denomination any advantage from getting control of public policy or the public purse. Those great ends I cannot but think are immeasurably compromised by today's decision.

Dissenting Opinion   MR. JUSTICE RUTLEDGE, with whom MR. JUSTICE FRANK-FURTER, MR. JUSTICE JACKSON and MR. JUSTICE BURTON agree, dissenting.

"Congress shall make no law respecting an establishment of religion, or prohibiting the free exercise thereof . . ." U.S. Const., Amend. I. . . .

Not simply an established church, but any law respecting an establishment of religion is forbidden. The Amendment was broadly but not loosely phrased. It is the compact and exact summation of its author's views formed during his long struggle for religious freedom. In Madison's own words characterizing Jefferson's Bill for Establishing Religious Freedom, the guaranty he put in our national charter, like the bill he piloted through the Virginia Assembly, was "a Model of technical precision, and perspicuous brevity." Madison could not have confused "church" and "religion," or "an established church" and "an establishment of religion." . . .

The reasons underlying the Amendment policy have not vanished with time or diminished in force. Now as when it was adopted the price of religious freedom is double. It is that the church and religion shall live both within and upon that freedom. There cannot be freedom of religion, safeguarded by the state, and intervention by the church or its agencies in the state's domain or dependency on its largesse. Madison's Remonstrance, Par. 6, 8. The great condition of religious liberty is that it be maintained free from sustenance, as also from other interferences, by the state. For when it comes to rest upon that secular foundation it vanishes with the resting. *Id.*, Par. 7, 8. Public money devoted to payment of religious costs, educational or other, brings the quest for more. It brings too the struggle of sect against sect for the larger share or for any. Here one by numbers alone will benefit most, there another. That is precisely the history of societies which have had an established religion and dissident groups. *Id.*, Par. 8, 11. It is the very thing Jefferson and Madison experienced and sought to guard against, whether in its blunt or in its more screened forms. *Ibid.* The end of such strife cannot be other than to destroy the cherished liberty. The dominating group will achieve the dominant benefit; or all will embroil the state in their dissensions. *Id.*, Par. 11. . . .

Two great drives are constantly in motion to abridge, in the name of education, the complete division of religion and civil authority which our forefathers made. One is to introduce religious education and observances into the public schools. The other, to obtain public funds for the aid and support of various private religious schools. See Johnson, The Legal Status of Church-State Relationships in the United States (1934); Thayer, Religion in Public Education (1947); Note (1941) 50 Yale L. J. 917. In my opinion both avenues were closed by the Constitution. Neither should be opened by this Court. The matter is not one of quantity, to be measured by the amount of money expended. Now as in Madison's day it is one of principle, to keep separate the separate spheres as the First Amendment drew them; to prevent the first experiment upon our liberties; and to keep the question from becoming entangled in corrosive precedents. We should not be less strict to keep strong and untarnished the one side of the shield of religious freedom than we have been of the other.

The judgment should be reversed.

BOARD OF EDUCATION v. ALLEN
392 U.S. 236 (1968)

MR. JUSTICE WHITE delivered the opinion of the Court.

A law of the State of New York requires local public school authorities to lend textbooks free of charge to all students in grades seven through 12; students attending private schools are included. This case presents the question whether this statute is a "law respecting an establishment of religion, or prohibiting the free exercise thereof," and so in conflict with the First and Fourteenth Amendments to the Constitution, because it authorizes the loan of textbooks to students attending parochial schools. We hold that the law is not in violation of the Constitution. . . .

Everson v. Board of Education, 330 U.S. 1 (1947), is the case decided by this Court that is most nearly in point for today's problem. New Jersey reimbursed parents for expenses incurred in busing their children to parochial schools. The Court stated that the Establishment Clause bars a State from passing "laws which aid one religion, aid all religions, or prefer one religion over another," and bars too any "tax in any amount, large or small . . . levied to support any religious activities or institutions, whatever they may be called, or whatever form they may adopt to teach or practice religion." 330 U.S., at 15–16. Nevertheless, said the Court, the Establishment Clause does not prevent a State from extending the benefits of state laws to all citizens without regard for their religious affiliation and does not prohibit "New Jersey from spending tax-raised funds to pay the bus fares of parochial school pupils as a part of a general program under which it pays the fares of pupils attending public and other schools." The statute was held to be valid even though one of its results was that "children are helped to get to church schools" and "some of the children might not be sent to the church schools if the parents were compelled to pay their children's bus fares out of their own pockets." 330 U.S. at 17. As with public provision of police and fire protection, sewage facilities, and streets and sidewalks, payment of bus fares was of some value to the religious school, but was nevertheless not such support of a religious institution as to be a prohibited establishment of religion within the meaning of the First Amendment.

Everson and later cases have shown that the line between state neutrality to religion and state support of religion is not easy to locate. "The constitutional standard is the separation of Church and State. The problem, like many problems in constitutional law, is one of degree." Zorach v. Clauson, 343 U.S. 306, 314 (1952). See McGowan v. Maryland, 366 U.S. 420 (1961). Based on Everson, Zorach, McGowan, and other cases, Abington School District v. Schempp, 374 U.S. 203 (1963), fashioned a test subscribed to by eight Justices for distinguishing between forbidden involvements of the State with religion and those contacts which the Establishment Clause permits:

> "The test may be stated as follows: what are the purpose and the primary effect of the enactment? If either is the advancement or inhibition of religion then the enactment exceeds the scope of legislative power as circumscribed by the Constitution. That is to say that to withstand the strictures of the Establishment Clause there must be a secular legislative purpose and a primary effect that neither advances nor inhibits religion. Everson v. Board of Education. . . ." 374 U.S., at 222.

This test is not easy to apply, but the citation of Everson by the Schempp Court to support its general standard made clear how the Schempp rule would be applied to the facts of Everson. The statute upheld in Everson would be considered a law having "a secular legislative purpose and a primary effect that neither advances nor inhibits religion." We reach the same result with respect to the New York law requiring school books to be loaned free of charge to all students in specified grades. The express purpose of §701 was stated by the New York Legislature to be furtherance of the educational opportunities available to the young. Appellants have shown us nothing about the necessary effects of the statute that is contrary to its stated purpose. The law merely makes available to all children the benefits of a general program to lend school books free of charge. Books are furnished at the request of the pupil and ownership remains, at least technically, in the State. Thus no funds or books are furnished to parochial schools, and the financial benefit is to parents and children, not to schools. Perhaps free books make it more likely that some children choose to attend a sectarian school, but that was true of the state-paid bus fares in

Everson and does not alone demonstrate an unconstitutional degree of support for a religious institution. . . .

The judgment is affirmed.

Concurring Opinion   MR. JUSTICE HARLAN, concurring.

Although I join the opinion and judgment of the Court, I wish to emphasize certain of the principles which I believe to be central to the determination of this case, and which I think are implicit in the Court's decision.

The attitude of government toward religion must, as this Court has frequently observed, be one of neutrality. Neutrality is, however, a coat of many colors. It requires that "government neither engage in nor compel religious practices, that it effect no favoritism among sects or between religion and nonreligion, and that it work deterrence of no religious belief." *Abington School District v. Schempp*, 374 U.S. 203, 305 (concurring opinion of Goldberg, J.). Realization of these objectives entails "no simple and clear measure," *id.*, at 306, by which this or any case may readily be decided; but these objectives do suggest the principles which I believe to be applicable in the present circumstances. I would hold that where the contested governmental activity is calculated to achieve nonreligious purposes otherwise within the competence of the State, and where the activity does not involve the State "so significantly and directly in the realm of the sectarian as to give rise to . . . divisive influences and inhibitions of freedom," *id.*, at 307, it is not forbidden by the religious clauses of the First Amendment.

In my opinion, §701 of the Education Law of New York does not employ religion as its standard for action or inaction, and is not otherwise inconsistent with these principles.

Dissenting Opinion   MR. JUSTICE BLACK, dissenting.

The Court here affirms a judgment of the New York Court of Appeals which sustained the constitutionality of a New York law providing state tax-raised funds to supply school books for use by pupils in schools owned and operated by religious sects. I believe the New York law held valid is a flat, flagrant, open violation of the First and Fourteenth Amendments which together forbid Congress or state legislatures to enact any law "respecting an establishment of religion." . . .

It is true, of course, that the New York law does not as yet formally adopt or establish a state religion. But it takes a great stride in that direction and coming events cast their shadows before them. The same powerful sectarian religious propagandists who have succeeded in securing passage of the present law to help religious schools carry on their sectarian religious purposes can and doubtless will continue their propaganda, looking toward complete domination and supremacy of their particular brand of religion. And it nearly always is by insidious approaches that the citadels of liberty are most successfully attacked.

I know of no prior opinion of this Court upon which the majority here can rightfully rely to support its holding this New York law constitutional. In saying this, I am not unmindful of the fact that the New York Court of Appeals purported to follow *Everson v. Board of Education, supra*, in which this Court, in an opinion written by me, upheld a New Jersey law authorizing reimbursement to parents for the transportation of children attending sectarian schools. That law did not attempt to deny the benefit of its general terms to children of any faith going to any legally authorized school. Thus, it was treated in the same way as a general law paying the streetcar fare of *all school children*, or a law providing midday lunches for all children or all school children, or a law to provide police protection for children going to and from school, or general laws to provide police and fire protection for buildings, including, of course, churches and church school buildings as well as others. . . .

I still subscribe to the belief that tax-raised funds cannot constitutionally be used to support religious schools, buy their school books, erect their buildings, pay their teachers, or pay any other of their maintenance expenses, even to the extent of one penny. The First Amendment's prohibition against governmental establishment of religion was written on the assumption that state aid to religion and religious schools generates discord, disharmony, hatred, and strife among our people, and that any government that supplies such aids is to that extent a tyranny. And I still believe that the only way to protect minority religious groups from majority groups in this country is to keep the wall of separation between church and state high and impregnable as the First and Fourteenth Amendments provide. The Court's affirmance here bodes nothing but evil to religious peace in this country.

Dissenting Opinion   MR. JUSTICE DOUGLAS, dissenting.

We have for review a statute which authorizes New York State to supply textbooks to students in parochial as well as in public schools. The New York Court of Appeals sustained the law on the grounds that it involves only "secular textbooks" and that that type of aid falls within *Everson v. Board of Education,* 330 U.S. 1, where a divided Court upheld a state law which made bus service available to students in parochial schools as well as to students in public schools. . . .

Whatever may be said of *Everson,* there is nothing ideological about a bus. There is nothing ideological about a school lunch, or a public nurse, or a scholarship. The constitutionality of such public aid to students in parochial schools turns on considerations not present in this textbook case. The textbook goes to the very heart of education in a parochial school. It is the chief, although not solitary, instrumentality for propagating a particular religious creed or faith. How can we possibly approve such state aid to a religion? . . .

It will be often difficult, as Mr. Justice Jackson said, to say "where the secular ends and the sectarian begins in education." *McCollum v. Board of Education*, 333 U.S., at 237–238. But certain it is that once the so-called "secular" textbook is the prize to be won by that religious faith which selects the book, the battle will be on for those positions of control. Judge Van Voorhis expressed the fear that in the end the state might dominate the church. Others fear that one sectarian group, gaining control of the state agencies which approve the "secular" textbooks, will use their control to disseminate ideas most congenial to their faith. It must be remembered that the very existence of the religious school—whether Catholic or Mormon, Presbyterian or Episcopalian—is to provide an education oriented to the dogma of the particular faith. . . .

These then are the battlegrounds where control of textbook distribution will be won or lost. Now that "secular" textbooks will pour into religious schools, we can rest assured that a contest will be on to provide those books for religious schools which the dominant religious group concludes best reflect the theocentric or other philosophy of the particular church.

The stakes are now extremely high—just as they were in the school prayer cases (see *Engel v. Vitale, supra*)—to obtain approval of what is "proper." For the "proper" books will radiate the "correct" religious view not only in the parochial school but in the public school as well.

Even if I am wrong in that basic premise, we still should not affirm the judgment below. Judge Van Voorhis, dissenting in the New York Court of Appeals, thought that the result of tying parochial school textbooks to public funds would be to put nonsectarian books into religious schools, which in the long view would tend towards state domination of the church. 20 N. Y. 2d, at 123, 228 N.E.2d, at 798, 281 N.Y.S.2d, at 810. That would, indeed, be the result if the school boards did not succumb to "sectarian" pressure or control. So, however the case be viewed—whether sectarian groups win control of school boards or do not gain such control—the principle of separation of church and state, inherent in the Establishment Clause of the First Amendment, is violated by what we today approve.

What Madison wrote in his famous Memorial and Remonstrance against Religious Assessments is highly pertinent here:

> "Who does not see that the same authority which can establish Christianity, in exclusion of all other Religions, may establish with the same ease any particular sect of Christians, in exclusion of all other Sects? That the

same authority which can force a citizen to contribute three pence only of his property for the support of any one establishment, may force him to conform to any other establishment in all cases whatsoever?"

DISCUSSION QUESTIONS

1. During the 1992 presidential campaign, President Bush argued that government should provide vouchers that parents could use to send their children to the private schools of their choice, whether religious or otherwise. Would these vouchers be constitutional, or would they violate the Establishment Clause as interpreted over four decades by the Supreme Court?

2. What is the difference between a tax deduction, a tax credit, and a direct payment from government?

3. What is the difference between lending textbooks directly to students and lending instructional materials directly to private religious schools?

4. Why is there less entanglement between government and a religious school if government pays for the construction of a building rather than for a salary supplement to teachers?

5. What is the difference between providing free transportation to all children regardless of destination and giving bus fare reimbursements to parents who pay to send their children to Catholic school?

6. How much weight should the Supreme Court justices give to the fact that if private religious schools close, the public school system would be overwhelmed with students?

7. How is providing financial support to religious schools like paying to build churches?

8. How important is it that the people who voted to place the First Amendment into the Constitution never thought about the issue of government support for religious schools?

CHAPTER
four
•••••••••

Symbols of Separation

•••••••••••••••••••••••••••••• DISCUSSION ••••••••••••••••••••••••••••••

The last two chapters focused on the extent to which governments establish religion by allowing prayer in public schools or by providing support for private religious schools. Governments can do other things that might be seen as providing support for religion in general, or for particular religious sects. Over the course of the last century, a number of Supreme Court decisions have examined this area.

RUNNING FREIGHT TRAINS ON SUNDAY

The case of *Hennington v. Georgia* was decided in 1896. At that time, in the state of Georgia it was illegal to run a freight train on Sunday, even if the train was simply passing through the state. The railroads argued that this law was unconstitutional because it interfered with interstate commerce, which should be subject to federal regulations, not state laws.

A majority of the Supreme Court justices did not agree. It had been illegal to work on Sunday in Georgia since 1762, and the justices saw the law prohibiting the running of freight trains as simply an extension of that principle. The Court decided that a state should have the power to declare a uniform day of rest for its citizens, even for those citizens who worked on the railroad. The issue of whether or not the Establishment Clause was violated was not explicitly raised in this case.

RELIGIOUS TESTS FOR HOLDING PUBLIC OFFICE

The Establishment Clause issue was raised in 1961, with the case of *Torcaso v. Watkins*. The case involved a provision in the laws of Maryland which stated that before people could hold public office, they had to swear that they believed in the existence of God. Because Mr. Torcaso refused to take the oath, he was denied the privilege of being a notary public.

The issue before the Court was: Could a state make holding public office conditional on a religious test, or did that violate the Establishment Clause? A unanimous Court ruled that this practice did violate the Establishment Clause. The Court thought that by requiring people who wished to hold public office to take such an oath, the state of Maryland was supporting a particular group of religions—those religions that believe in the existence of one supreme god. By forcing people who wanted to hold public office to swear that they believed in this one god, the government was encouraging people to have such beliefs, which also violated the Establishment Clause. The Maryland law also inter-fered with Mr. Torcaso's freedom to believe whatever he wanted, in violation of the Free Exercise Clause.

The *Torcaso* decision was easy for the Court. Here was a decision supported by both the Establishment Clause and the Free Exercise Clause of the First Amendment. Here was a practice that the authors of the First Amendment probably did have in mind when they voted to place the amendment into the U.S. Constitution, and a practice expressly forbidden by the Bill for Establish-ing Religious Freedom in Virginia. By limiting government employment to those who held particular religious beliefs, government was encouraging people to hold and express those particular beliefs.

SUNDAY CLOSING LAWS

Also in 1961, the Court faced a much more difficult decision with the case of *McGowan v. Maryland*. The issue in this case was whether states could make it illegal for some businesses to operate on Sundays. Laws that either made the operation of some kinds of businesses illegal on Sunday or outlawed the selling of some kinds of products on Sunday were commonly called Sunday closing laws, and most states had some form of Sunday closing law on the books. Mr. McGowan was convicted of selling a loose-leaf binder, a can of floor wax, a stapler, some staples, and a toy on a Sunday.

Chief Justice Warren, who wrote the majority opinion, stated that the purpose of this Maryland law was to establish a uniform day of rest for all working people. He quoted Blackstone, who wrote in the 1700s:

> The keeping one day in seven holy, as a time of relaxation and refreshment as well as for public worship, is of admirable service to a state considered

merely as a civil institution. It humanizes, by the help of conversation and society, the manners of the lower classes, which would otherwise degenerate into a sordid ferocity, and savage selfishness of spirit; it enables the industrious workman to pursue his occupation in the ensuing week with health and cheerfulness.

The chief justice was impressed by the fact that labor unions as well as religious groups supported these kinds of laws. A majority of the justices believed that this law was not a violation of the Establishment Clause, and that the states had the power to control business and commerce within their borders.

As the lone dissenting justice, Justice Douglas argued that this law violated both the Establishment Clause and the Free Exercise Clause. By choosing Sunday, the Sabbath of a particular group of religions, as the common day of rest, the state had given encouragement to, and shown support for, a particular group of religions, and so, Justice Douglas believed, violated the Establishment Clause. At the same time, he felt that this law interfered with the religious freedom of many people who belonged to religions that held some other day as the Sabbath. These people would be at a disadvantage in business because they could not work on their own Sabbath and also on the official day of rest, Sunday. He asked what compelling reason the states could put forth to justify this interference with religious freedom. The answer appeared to be convenience: it was convenient if everyone had the same day off each week. Justice Douglas did not believe that convenience justified this violation of the First Amendment.

The rest of the justices believed that states must be able to regulate business, and that requiring a common day of rest once a week was simply an effort to regulate business. While Sunday did coincide with the Sabbath of some religions, any day of the week might be seen as having some religious significance to some group. Choosing a common day of rest that also coincided with the Sabbath of the majority of citizens seemed reasonable under the circumstances.

These justices did not feel that this law would actually cause anyone to change their religion. People who hold other days sacred already have to face a number of inconveniences, and the Sunday closing laws did not significantly increase those inconveniences. Also, any closing law would be an inconvenience for somebody. For example, a law forcing all merchants to close on Saturdays would give Jewish merchants a commercial advantage, because Saturday coincides with the Jewish Sabbath. In other words, any decision the Court could come up with would affect some religious groups positively and other religious groups negatively. That being the case, the Court decided to simply go along with the wishes of the various state legislatures.

In the 1970s many states significantly altered their Sunday closing laws, in most cases allowing all businesses to stay open on Sunday and to sell most kinds of merchandise. This led to another problem. In 1977 the state of Connecticut revised its Sunday closing laws, allowing most stores to stay open on Sunday. Many legislators thought that this might cause a hardship for employees who could not work on Sunday because of their religious beliefs. To solve this problem, the Connecticut legislature passed a law requiring all businesses to give their employees one day off a week to observe their Sabbath. A Presbyterian man, Donald Thornton, was fired because he refused to work on Sunday. He sued his employer under the Connecticut law, and the case went to the Connecticut Supreme Court (*Thornton v. Caldor*). The Connecticut Supreme Court declared the new law to be unconstitutional as a violation of the Establishment Clause of the U.S. Constitution. The Connecticut Supreme Court believed that this law could not pass the *Lemon* test because the law had no clear "secular purpose," and it had the primary effect of advancing religion.

The case was then appealed to the U.S. Supreme Court. Eight of the nine justices of the U.S. Supreme Court agreed that this Connecticut law violated the Establishment Clause. Chief Justice Burger, in writing the majority opinion, agreed with the Connecticut Supreme Court that the *Lemon* test had been violated. The only real purpose of this new law was to grant a privilege to people who observed a Sabbath.

Justice O'Connor wrote her own concurring opinion, which was joined by Justice Marshall. She argued that the *Lemon* test should be abandoned, because it did not provide much real guidance in these cases. She suggested that the real question should be whether a law appears to convey a "message of endorsement" of particular religions or religion in general. In this case, the Connecticut law clearly did just that. People who hold a particular day to be a holy day had been singled out by the Connecticut law for a special privilege; this privilege was not granted to nonreligious people who did not have a Sabbath day.

Some critics argued that this decision did not make sense. Why was it constitutional to require all businesses to close on Sunday, the Sabbath for most Christians, but it was not constitutional to allow business to be open on Sunday and require them to allow employees to have their Sabbath off, regardless of which day of the week that happened to be?

The answer revolves around the question of "secular purpose." The Court could accept the idea that one purpose of a Sunday closing law was to guarantee that everyone in the society would get a day off once a week to rest. This law would apply to everyone equally, the religious and the nonreligious. When this law was repealed and replaced with a law that forced employers to give their employees their Sabbath as a day of rest, there was no longer a secular purpose to the law; it was simply a privilege granted to the religious. Also, the nonreligious could no longer take advantage of this privilege. This meant that anyone who wanted a day off in Connecticut would be encouraged to join a religious sect that observed a Sabbath. This could be seen as a type of encouragement of religion. Most justices of the U.S. Supreme Court agreed that this was what the Establishment Clause was designed to prevent.

REGISTRATION OF RELIGIONS AS CHARITIES

The case of *Larson v. Valente* involved a Minnesota law that required any religion that received over 50 percent of its funds from nonmembers to register with the state as a charity and be subject to all the regulations charities had to comply with, including allowing the state to examine their books. In practice this meant that mainstream religions did not have to comply with the law, while smaller, newer sects, such as the Unification Church, which brought this lawsuit, would have to comply. In 1982 the Court ruled five to four that this law was an unconstitutional violation of the Establishment Clause because "the clearest command of the Establishment Clause is that one religious denomination cannot be officially preferred over another."

Minnesota argued that it had a right and a duty to protect its citizens from everyone who asked for money for a supposed charitable purpose, including religions. The state argued that religions that obtained most of their funds by begging on the street were clearly different from religions that raised most of their funds from member contributions. A majority of the Supreme Court justices did not agree, because in practice, this distinction meant that one set of rules applied to the mainstream religions, while another set of regulations applied to newer sects. By providing government support for one group of religions and punishing another group of religions, the Minnesota law violated the Establishment Clause. These justices also believed that the Free Exercise Clause was involved in this case, because people who wanted to belong to, or contribute to, new religions would be discouraged from doing so because of this government oversight and regulation.

Four justices dissented in this case, not because they disagreed with the logic of the majority, but because they were not convinced that the Unification Church was really a religion. In their opinion, the case should have been sent back to Minnesota for a judge to rule on that question before any decisions could be made on the constitutional question.

GOVERNMENTAL DECISION-MAKING POWER

A 1982 case, *Larkin v. Grendel's Den*, concerned a Massachusetts statute that prohibited issuing a liquor license to any establishment within 500 feet of a church if the church in question objected. All but one of the justices could agree that the law in question was unconstitutional. The justices had no problem with the idea that government could control the issuing of liquor licenses, but they objected to the idea that in this case the decision about whether a liquor license would be issued was essentially left up to a religious group. The church had been put in the position of making a governmental decision, and the granting of governmental decision-making power to churches violated the Establishment Clause.

PRAYER IN LEGISLATURES

The next year found the Court divided six to three over whether or not state legislatures could open their legislative sessions each day with a prayer from an official chaplain (*Marsh v. Chambers*). The particular legislature in question, Nebraska, had a Presbyterian minister as chaplain who said a prayer each day the legislature was in session. A majority of the members of the Court found that this practice did not violate the Establishment Clause. For centuries state legislatures and the U.S. Congress have had paid chaplains to recite prayers at the beginning of legislative sessions. The people who voted to place the First Amendment into the Constitution engaged in this practice the day before and the day after they voted to do so, which suggests that they did not believe that the First Amendment made this practice illegal. From as far back as we have written records, lawgivers had invoked their gods to give them guidance in writing law. Even U.S. Supreme Court sessions are opened with the words "God save the United States and this Honorable Court."

The Court majority was also mindful of the strictly ceremonial effect of these prayers. The prayers lend an air of solemnity to the occasion. These justices did not believe that anyone listening to the prayers would be moved to change his or her mind about anything or to see these ceremonial prayers as any kind of "real" support for religion in general or for one religion in particular. Because these prayers were part of ceremonies that went back many centuries, the justices did not consider them a threat to the religious peace of the republic.

The three dissenting justices pointed out that before the advent of the First Amendment every society that had existed on earth had followed the dictates of an established church. The American experiment was the first attempt to create and govern a society without a common set of religious beliefs. These dissenters were not surprised that it did not occur to the congressmen and legislators who voted for the First Amendment that having a chaplain say a prayer every day might violate the Establishment Clause. The dissenters were also not impressed by the argument that the legislators hearing the prayer would probably not be moved by it. They were more concerned that anyone sitting in the gallery, seeing this religious ceremony performed in the seat of government every day at public expense, would find this to be an endorsement of a particular religion.

NATIVITY DISPLAYS

In 1984 and 1989 the Court had to examine the nature and makeup of government Christmas displays. The first case, *Lynch v. Donnelly* (see p. 65), involved a Christian nativity scene that was part of a large Christmas display in Pawtucket, Rhode Island. The nativity scene and the other Christmas displays were owned by the government but displayed on private land. The Court split on this decision, with four justices in favor of the display, four against the display, and Justice O'Connor as the swing vote.

The four in favor argued that total separation between the church and the state is not possible, and that some accommodation must be made for the fact that Americans are a religious people. The other four justices thought that for a city to own a nativity scene clearly violated the Establishment Clause. That left the decision up to Justice O'Connor. She argued that the key in these kinds of cases should be whether or not government would be seen as endorsing a particular religion. She believed that would not happen in this case, because she saw the display as a kind of outdoor museum and found no real message of endorsement.

Five years later, with *Allegheny County v. A.C.L.U.* (see p. 70), Justice O'Connor found a nativity display that she believed did convey a message of endorsement of religion by government, so what had been five to four in favor of the Pawtucket display became five to four against the Allegheny display. What was the difference? Allegheny County had placed a large nativity scene at the bottom of the grand staircase in the middle of the courthouse. The nativity scene was not out in a park surrounded by other displays of the winter season; it was standing alone inside a government building. Justice O'Connor thought that this location did convey a message that government endorsed a particular religion, in this case Christianity, and for this reason the nativity scene violated the Establishment Clause.

Justice Kennedy, writing for the dissenting justices in the *Allegheny* case, argued that government should be allowed to acknowledge and support religion because religion is an accepted part of the cultural heritage of the United States. He believed that the First Amendment should allow governments to recognize the central role religion plays in the lives of most Americans. He also argued that a very high wall of separation between church and state would send a message that government disapproves of religion in general, and that this would be just as bad as sending a message of approval.

A majority of the justices were not swayed by these arguments. They thought that a nativity scene in the middle of a government building could only be seen as an endorsement of a particular religion and was no more permissible than any other religious symbol would be if placed in such a prominent place in a government building.

CONCLUSION

When it comes to cases involving religious symbols the U.S. Supreme Court has followed a path similar to the path it has taken concerning government support for religious schools. The Court has avoided creating a very high wall of separation and has instead tried to allow some accommodation between government and religion. A nativity scene as part of a winter display containing many different kinds of religious symbols is permissible, because it does not convey too great a message of endorsement of religion in general or of a particular group of religions. On the other hand, a symbol of Christianity in the middle of a government building does create too strong a message of endorsement of a particular religion and is therefore a violation of the Establishment Clause.

The Court has been willing to allow certain governmental ceremonies to contain a religious element in recognition of the long tradition involved in those ceremonies. The U.S. Congress and state legislatures are allowed to begin the day with a prayer because this has been going on for centuries and is motivated more by respect for tradition than by any desire to convert people from one religion to another.

Laws that, in the opinion of the Court, might really encourage someone to join a religion violate the Establishment Clause. The Maryland law that required those seeking public office to swear that they believed in God clearly violated the Establishment Clause, because it required people to become religious in order to receive this government benefit. The same is true of the Connecticut law that granted a day off once a week to those who observed a Sabbath. A law giving everyone one day off a week could be seen as an effort to guarantee that all citizens will be able to maintain their health. If this law is replaced with a law that allows the religious to have their Sabbath day off, but does not give the same privilege to the nonreligious, the Establishment Clause has been violated, because this law might encourage people to join religious sects that observed a Sabbath in order to have a day off.

The Supreme Court has been forced to distinguish between activities that it feels are real violations of the Establishment Clause and activities that a majority of the justices do not believe really show support for particular religions. The Court has acknowledged that, given the history of the United States, it would be impossible to remove every aspect of religion from the activities of government. The Court has tried instead to outlaw only those practices that it thought were a serious threat to the religious neutrality of government. This middle-of-the-road approach has left many people unhappy with Court decisions. At the same time, both sides of this issue have been able to claim victory from time to time.

CASE DECISIONS

Lynch v. Donnelly, decided in 1984, and *Allegheny County v. A.C.L.U.*, decided in 1989, are concerned with when a government may display a Christian nativity scene. In both cases, four justices expressed the opinion that government-sponsored nativity scenes would always be unconstitutional, while four justices believed these nativity scenes would always be constitutional. This left both decisions up to Justice O'Connor, who allowed the nativity scene in the *Lynch* case but not in the *Allegheny* case. The majority and dissenting opinions are included here, along with Justice O'Connor's concurring opinion in each case.

Following are excerpts from the case decisions.

∗ ∗ ∗ ∗ ∗ ∗ ∗ ∗ ∗ ∗

LYNCH v. DONNELLY
465 U.S. 668 (1984)

CHIEF JUSTICE BURGER delivered the opinion of the Court.

We granted certiorari to decide whether the Establishment Clause of the First Amendment prohibits a municipality from including a crèche, or Nativity scene, in its annual Christmas display.

Each year, in cooperation with the downtown retail merchants' association, the city of Pawtucket, R. I., erects a Christmas display as part of its observance of the Christmas holiday season. The display is situated in a park owned by a nonprofit organization and located in the heart of the shopping district. The display is essentially like those to be found in hundreds of towns or cities across the Nation—often on public grounds—during the Christmas season. The Pawtucket display comprises many of the figures and decorations traditionally associated with Christmas, including, among other things, a Santa Claus house, reindeer pulling Santa's sleigh, candy-striped poles, a Christmas tree, carolers, cut-out figures representing such characters as a clown, an elephant, and a teddy bear, hundreds of colored lights, a large banner that reads "SEASONS GREETINGS," and the crèche at issue here. All components of this display are owned by the city.

The crèche, which has been included in the display for 40 or more years, consists of the traditional figures, including the Infant Jesus, Mary and Joseph, angels, shepherds, kings, and animals, all ranging in height from 5" to 5'. In 1973, when the present crèche was acquired, it cost the city $1,365; it now is valued at $200. The erection and dismantling of the crèche costs the city about $20 per year; nominal expenses are incurred in lighting the crèche. No money has been expended on its maintenance for the past 10 years. . . .

This Court has explained that the purpose of the Establishment and Free Exercise Clauses of the First Amendment is

> "to prevent, as far as possible, the intrusion of either [the church or the state] into the precincts of the other." *Lemon v. Kurtzman*, 403 U.S. 602, 614 (1971).

At the same time, however, the Court has recognized that

> "total separation is not possible in an absolute sense. Some relationship between government and religious organizations is inevitable." *Ibid.*

In every Establishment Clause case, we must reconcile the inescapable tension between the objective of preventing unnecessary intrusion of either the church or the state upon the other, and the reality that, as the Court has so often noted, total separation of the two is not possible. . . .

Art galleries supported by public revenues display religious paintings of the 15th and 16th centuries, predominantly inspired by one religious faith. The National Gallery in Washington, maintained with Government support, for example, has long exhibited masterpieces with religious messages, notably the Last Supper, and paintings depicting the Birth of Christ, the Crucifixion, and the Resurrection, among many others with explicit Christian themes and messages. The very chamber in which oral arguments on this case were heard is decorated with a notable and permanent—not seasonal—symbol of religion: Moses with the Ten Commandments. Congress has long provided chapels in the Capitol for religious worship and meditation. . . .

The narrow question is whether there is a secular purpose for Pawtucket's display of the crèche. The display is sponsored by the city to celebrate the Holiday and to depict the origins of that Holiday. These are legitimate secular purposes. . . .

The dissent asserts some observers may perceive that the city has aligned itself with the Christian faith by including a Christian symbol in its display and that this serves to advance religion. We can assume, *arguendo*, that the display advances religion in a sense; but our precedents plainly contemplate that on occasion some advancement of religion will result from governmental action.

The Court has made it abundantly clear, however, that "not every law that confers an 'indirect,' 'remote,' or 'incidental' benefit upon [religion] is, for that reason alone, constitutionally invalid." *Nyquist*, 413 U.S., at 771; see also *Widmar v. Vincent*, 454 U.S. 263, 273 (1981). Here, whatever benefit there is to one faith or religion or to all religions, is indirect, remote, and incidental; display of the crèche is no more an advancement or endorsement of religion than the Congressional and Executive recognition of the origins of the Holiday itself as "Christ's Mass," or the exhibition of literally hundreds of religious paintings in governmentally supported museums. . . .

We hold that, notwithstanding the religious significance of the crèche, the city of Pawtucket has not violated the Establishment Clause of the First Amendment. Accordingly, the judgment of the Court of Appeals is reversed.

It is so ordered.

Concurring Opinion   JUSTICE O'CONNOR, concurring.

I concur in the opinion of the Court. I write separately to suggest a clarification of our Establishment Clause doctrine. The suggested approach leads to the same result in this case as that taken by the Court, and the Court's opinion, as I read it, is consistent with my analysis.

The Establishment Clause prohibits government from making adherence to a religion relevant in any way to a person's standing in the political community. Government can run afoul of that prohibition in two principal ways. One is excessive entanglement with religious institutions, which may interfere with the independence of the institutions, give the institutions access to government or governmental powers not fully shared by nonadherents of the religion, and foster the creation of political constituencies defined along religious lines. E.g., *Larkin v. Grendel's Den, Inc.*, 459 U.S. 116 (1982). The second and more direct infringement is government endorsement or disapproval of religion. Endorsement sends a message to nonadherents that they are outsiders, not full members of the political community, and an accompanying message to adherents that they are insiders, favored members of the political community. Disapproval sends the opposite message. See generally *Abington School District v. Schempp*, 374 U.S. 203 (1963).

Our prior cases have used the three-part test articulated in *Lemon v. Kurtzman*, 403 U.S. 602, 612–613 (1971), as a guide to detecting these two forms of unconstitutional government action. It has never been entirely clear, however, how the three parts of the test relate to the principles enshrined in the Establishment Clause. Focusing on institutional entanglement and on endorsement or disapproval of religion clarifies the *Lemon* test as an analytical device. . . .

Applying that formulation to this case, I would find that Pawtucket did not intend to convey any message of endorsement of Christianity or disapproval of non-Christian religions. The evident purpose of including the crèche in the larger display was not promotion of the religious content of the crèche but celebration of the public holiday through its traditional symbols. Celebration of public holidays, which have cultural significance even if they also have religious aspects, is a legitimate secular purpose. . . .

Pawtucket's display of its crèche, I believe, does not communicate a message that the government intends to endorse the Christian beliefs represented by the crèche. Although the religious and indeed sectarian significance of the crèche, as the District Court found, is not neutralized by the setting, the overall holiday setting changes what viewers may fairly understand to be the purpose of the display—as a typical museum setting, though not neutralizing the religious content of a religious painting, negates any message of endorsement of that content. The display celebrates a public holiday, and no one contends that declaration of that holiday is understood to be an endorsement of religion. The holiday itself has very strong secular components and traditions. Government celebration of the holiday, which is extremely common, generally is not understood to endorse the religious content of the holiday, just as government celebration of Thanksgiving is not so understood. The crèche is a traditional symbol of the holiday that is very commonly displayed along with purely secular symbols, as it was in Pawtucket. . . .

The city of Pawtucket is alleged to have violated the Establishment Clause by endorsing the Christian beliefs represented by the crèche included in its Christmas display. Giving the challenged practice the careful scrutiny it deserves, I cannot say that the particular crèche display at issue in this case was intended to endorse or had the effect of endorsing Christianity. I agree with the Court that the judgment below must be reversed.

Dissenting Opinion   JUSTICE BRENNAN, with whom JUSTICE MARSHALL, JUSTICE BLACKMUN, and JUSTICE STEVENS join, dissenting.

The principles announced in the compact phrases of the Religion Clauses have as the Court today reminds us, . . . proved difficult to apply. Faced with that uncertainty, the Court properly looks for guidance to the settled test announced in *Lemon v. Kurtzman*, 403 U.S. 602 (1971), for assessing whether a challenged governmental practice involves an impermissible step toward the establishment of religion. . . . Applying that test to this case, the Court reaches an essentially narrow result which turns largely upon the particular holiday context in which the city of Pawtucket's nativity scene appeared. The Court's decision implicitly leaves open questions concerning the constitutionality of the public display on public property of a crèche standing alone, or the public display of other distinctively religious symbols such as a cross. Despite the narrow contours of the Court's opinion, our precedents in my view compel the holding that Pawtucket's inclusion of a life-sized display depicting the biblical description of the birth of Christ as part of its annual Christmas celebration is unconstitutional. Nothing in the history of such practices or the setting in which the city's crèche is presented obscures or diminishes the plain fact that Pawtucket's action amounts to an impermissible governmental endorsement of a particular faith. . . .

The essence of the creche's symbolic purpose and effect is to prompt the observer to experience a sense of simple awe and wonder appropriate to the contemplation of one of the central elements of Christian dogma—that God sent His Son into the world to be a Messiah. Contrary to the Court's suggestion, the crèche is far from a mere representation of a "particular historic religious event." . . . It is, instead, best understood as a mystical re-creation of an event that lies at the heart of Christian faith. To suggest, as the Court does, that such a symbol is merely "traditional" and therefore no different from Santa's house or reindeer is not only offensive to those for whom the crèche has profound significance, but insulting to those who insist for religious or personal reasons that the story of Christ is in no sense a part of "history" nor an unavoidable element of our national "heritage."

For these reasons, the crèche in this context simply cannot be viewed as playing the same role that an ordinary museum display does. . . . The Court seems to assume that prohibiting Pawtucket from displaying a crèche would be tantamount to prohibiting a state college from including the Bible or Milton's Paradise Lost in a course on English literature. But in those cases the religiously inspired materials are being considered solely as literature. The purpose is plainly not to single out the particular religious beliefs that may have inspired the authors, but to see in these writings the outlines of a larger imaginative universe shared with other forms of literary expression. The same may be said of a course devoted to the study of art; when the course turns to Gothic architecture, the emphasis is not on the religious beliefs which the cathedrals exalt, but rather upon the "aesthetic consequences of [such religious] thought." . . .

Under our constitutional scheme, the role of safeguarding our "religious heritage" and of promoting religious beliefs is reserved as the exclusive prerogative of our Nation's churches, religious institutions, and spiritual leaders. Because the Framers of the Establishment Clause understood that "religion is too personal, too sacred, too holy to permit its 'unhallowed perversion' by civil [authorities]," *Engel v. Vitale*, 370 U.S., at 432, the Clause demands that government play no role in this effort. The Court today brushes aside these concerns by insisting that Pawtucket has done nothing more than include a "traditional" symbol of Christmas in its celebration of this national holiday, thereby muting the religious content of the crèche. . . . But the city's action should be recognized for what it is: a coercive, though perhaps small, step toward establishing the sectarian preferences of the majority at the expense of the minority, accomplished by placing public facilities and funds in support of the religious symbolism and theological tidings that the crèche conveys. As Justice Frankfurter, writing in *McGowan v. Maryland*, observed, the Establishment Clause "withdr[aws] from the sphere of legitimate legislative concern and competence a specific, but comprehensive, area of human conduct: man's belief or disbelief in the verity of some transcendental idea and man's expression in action of that belief or disbelief." 366 U.S., at 465–466 (separate opinion). That the Constitution sets this realm of thought and feeling apart from the pressures and antagonisms of government is one of its supreme achievements. Regrettably, the Court today tarnishes that achievement.

I dissent.

ALLEGHENY COUNTY v. A.C.L.U.
492 U.S. 573 (1989)

JUSTICE BLACKMUN announced the judgment of the Court. . . .

This litigation concerns the constitutionality of . . . a crèche placed on the Grand Staircase of the Allegheny County Courthouse. . . .

The County Courthouse is owned by Allegheny County and is its seat of government. It houses the offices of the County Commissioners, Controller, Treasurer, Sheriff, and Clerk of Court. Civil and criminal trials are held there. The "main," "most beautiful," and "most public" part of the courthouse is its Grand Staircase, set into one arch and surrounded by others, with arched windows serving as a backdrop. . . .

Since 1981, the county has permitted the Holy Name society, a Roman Catholic group, to display a crèche in the County Courthouse during the Christmas holiday season. . . . Christmas, we note perhaps needlessly, is the holiday when Christians celebrate the birth of Jesus of Nazareth, whom they believe to be the Messiah. Western churches have celebrated Christmas Day on December 25 since the fourth century. As observed in this Nation, Christmas has a secular as well as a religious dimension. . . .

We have had occasion in the past to apply Establishment Clause principles to the government's display of objects with religious significance. In *Stone v. Graham*, 449 U.S. 39 (1980), we held that the display of a copy of the Ten

Commandments on the walls of public classrooms violates the Establishment Clause. Closer to the facts of this litigation is *Lynch v. Donnelly, supra*, in which we considered whether the city of Pawtucket, R.I., had violated the Establishment Clause by including a crèche in its annual Christmas display, located in a private park within the downtown shopping district. By a 5–4 decision in that difficult case, the Court upheld inclusion of the crèche in the Pawtucket display, holding, *inter alia*, that the inclusion of the crèche did not have the impermissible effect of advancing or promoting religion.

The rationale of the majority opinion in *Lynch* is none too clear: the opinion contains two strands, neither of which provides guidance for decision in subsequent cases. First, the opinion states that the inclusion of the crèche in the display was "no more an advancement or endorsement of religion" than other "endorsements" this Court has approved in the past, 465 U.S., at 683, 104 S.Ct., at 1364—but the opinion offers no discernible measure for distinguishing between permissible and impermissible endorsements. Second, the opinion observes that any benefit the government's display of the crèche gave to religion was no more than "indirect, remote, and incidental," *ibid.*—without saying how or why.

Although Justice O'Connor joined the majority opinion in *Lynch*, she wrote a concurrence that differs in significant respects from the majority opinion. The main difference is that the concurrence provides a sound analytical framework for evaluating governmental use of religious symbols.

First and foremost, the concurrence squarely rejects any notion that this Court will tolerate some government endorsement of religion. Rather, the concurrence recognizes any endorsement of religion as "invalid," *id.*, at 690, because it "sends a message to nonadherents that they are outsiders, not full members of the political community, and an accompanying message to adherents that they are insiders, favored members of the political community." *Id.*, at 688.

Second, the concurrence articulates a method for determining whether the government's use of an object with religious meaning has the effect of endorsing religion. The effect of the display depends upon the message that the government's practice communicates: the question is "what viewers may fairly understand to be the purpose of the display." *Id.*, at 692. That inquiry, of necessity, turns upon the context in which the contested object appears: "a typical museum setting, though not neutralizing the religious content of a religious painting, negates any message of endorsement of that content." *Ibid.* The concurrence thus emphasizes that the constitutionality of the crèche in that case depended upon its "particular physical setting," *ibid.*, and further observes: "Every government practice must be judged in its unique circumstances to determine whether it [endorses] religion." *Id.*, at 694. . . .

Under the Court's holding in Lynch, the effect of a crèche display turns on its setting. Here, unlike in Lynch, nothing in the context of the display detracts from the crèche's religious message. The Lynch display comprised a series of figures and objects, each group of which had its own focal point. Santa's house and his reindeer were objects of attention separate from the crèche, and had their specific visual story to tell. Similarly, whatever a "talking" wishing well may be, it obviously was a center of attention separate from the crèche. Here, in contrast, the crèche stands alone: it is the single element of the display on the Grand Staircase. . . .

Furthermore, the crèche sits on the Grand Staircase, the "main" and "most beautiful part" of the building that is the seat of county government. . . . No viewer could reasonably think that it occupies this location without the support and approval of the government. Thus, by permitting the "display of the crèche in this particular physical setting," Lynch, 465 U.S., at 692 (O'Connor, J., concurring), the county sends an unmistakable message that it supports and promotes the Christian praise to God that is the crèche's religious message. . . .

In sum, Lynch teaches that government may celebrate Christmas in some manner and form, but not in a way that endorses Christian doctrine. Here, Allegheny County has transgressed this line. It has chosen to celebrate Christmas in a way that has the effect of endorsing a patently Christian message: Glory to God for the birth of Jesus Christ. Under Lynch, and the rest of our cases, nothing more is required to demonstrate a violation of the Establishment Clause. The display of the crèche in this context, therefore, must be permanently enjoined. . . .

It is so ordered.

Concurring Opinion   JUSTICE O'CONNOR, concurring in part and concurring in the judgment.

Judicial review of government action under the Establishment Clause is a delicate task. The Court has avoided drawing lines which entirely sweep away all government recognition and acknowledgment of the role of religion in the lives of our citizens for to do so would exhibit not neutrality but hostility to religion. . . . Unfortunately, even the development of articulable standards and guidelines has not always resulted in agreement among the Members of this Court on the results in individual cases. And so it is again today. . . .

I joined the majority opinion in Lynch because, as I read that opinion, it was consistent with the analysis set forth in my separate concurrence, which stressed that "[e]very government practice must be judged in its *unique circumstances* to determine whether it constitutes an endorsement or disapproval of religion." Id., at 694 (emphasis added). Indeed, by referring repeatedly to "inclusion of the crèche" in the larger holiday display, *id.*, at 671, 680–682, 686, the *Lynch* majority recognized that the crèche had to be viewed in light of the total display of which it was a part. Moreover, I joined the Court's discussion in Part II of *Lynch* concerning government acknowledgments of religion in American life because, in my view, acknowledgments such as the legislative prayers upheld in *Marsh v. Chambers*, 463 U.S. 783 (1983), and the printing of "In God We Trust" on our coins serve the secular purposes of "solemnizing public occasions, expressing confidence in the future and encouraging the recognition of what is worthy of appreciation in society." *Lynch*, 465 U.S., at 693 (concurring opinion). Because they serve such secular purposes and because of their "history and ubiquity," such government acknowledgments of religion are not understood as conveying an endorsement of particular religious beliefs. *Ibid.* At the same time, it is clear that "[g]overnment practices that purport to celebrate or acknowledge events with religious significance must be subjected to careful judicial scrutiny." . . .

For the reasons stated in Part IV of the Court's opinion in this case, I agree that the crèche displayed on the Grand Staircase of the Allegheny County Courthouse, the seat of county government, conveys a message to nonadherents of Christianity that they are not full members of the political community, and a corresponding message to Christians that they are favored members of the political community. In contrast to the crèche in *Lynch*, which was displayed in a private park in the city's commercial district as part of a broader display of traditional secular symbols of the holiday season, this crèche stands alone in the County Courthouse. The display of religious symbols in public areas of core government buildings runs a special risk of "mak[ing] religion relevant, in reality or public perception, to status in the political community." . . . The Court correctly concludes that placement of the central religious symbol of the Christmas holiday season at the Allegheny County Courthouse has the unconstitutional effect of conveying a government endorsement of Christianity.

Dissenting Opinion   JUSTICE KENNEDY, with whom THE CHIEF JUSTICE, JUSTICE WHITE, and JUSTICE SCALIA join, . . . dissenting in part.

The majority holds that the County of Allegheny violated the Establishment Clause by displaying a crèche in the county courthouse, because the "principal or primary effect" of the display is to advance religion within the meaning of *Lemon v. Kurtzman*, 403 U.S. 602, 612–613 (1971). This view of the Establishment Clause reflects an unjustified hostility toward religion, a hostility inconsistent with our history and our precedents, and I dissent from this holding. . . .

If government is to participate in its citizens' celebration of a holiday that contains both a secular and a religious component, enforced recognition of only the secular aspect would signify the callous indifference toward religious faith that our cases and traditions do not require; for by commemorating the holiday only as it is celebrated by nonadherents, the government would be refusing to acknowledge the plain fact, and the historical reality, that many of its citizens celebrate its religious aspects as well. Judicial invalidation of government's attempts to recognize the religious underpinnings of the holiday would signal not neutrality but a pervasive intent to insulate government from all things religious. The Religion Clauses do not require government to acknowledge these holidays or their religious component; but our strong tradition of government accommodation and acknowledgment permits government to do so. . . .

The suit before us is admittedly a troubling one. It must be conceded that, however neutral the purpose of the city and county, the eager proselytizer may seek to use these symbols for his own ends. The urge to use them to teach or to taunt is always present. It is also true that some devout adherents of Judaism or Christianity may be as offended by the holiday display as are nonbelievers, if not more so. To place these religious symbols in a common hallway or sidewalk, where they may be ignored or even insulted, must be distasteful to many who cherish their meaning.

For these reasons, I might have voted against installation of these particular displays were I a local legislative official. But we have no jurisdiction over matters of taste within the realm of constitutionally permissible discretion. Our role is enforcement of a written Constitution. In my view, the principles of the Establishment Clause and our Nation's historic traditions of diversity and pluralism allow communities to make reasonable judgments respecting the accommodation or acknowledgment of holidays with both cultural and religious aspects. No constitutional violation occurs when they do so by displaying a symbol of the holiday's religious origins.

DISCUSSION QUESTIONS

1. If it is illegal to place a nativity scene inside a courthouse and legal to place a nativity scene in a private park along with other religious symbols, do you think that it would be legal to place a nativity scene on the front lawn of the courthouse if other symbols of the winter season were included in the display?

2. The Connecticut law guaranteeing everyone one day off a week to observe their Sabbath was unconstitutional. Could Connecticut replace this law with a law that says every employee must be given one day off a week, and the employee must be allowed to choose the day?

3. It is constitutional for a legislature to begin each day with a short prayer. Would it be constitutional for a legislature to begin each day with a sermon from a Christian minister?

4. It is unconstitutional to ask people to swear that they believe in God before they can hold public office. Some religions forbid taking any kind of oath. Would it be constitutional to require people to take an oath that they support the Constitution of the United States before they can hold public office?

5. The U.S. Supreme Court has tried to distinguish between accommodation of religion on the one hand, which is acceptable, and support for religion on the other hand, which is unacceptable. Do you think the Court has been successful?

6. A Christmas tree is a symbol of Christianity. Do you think it is a violation of the Establishment Clause for public schools to have Christmas trees in their classrooms?

7. Do you think the fact that money in the United States says "In God We Trust" violates the Establishment Clause?

CHAPTER
five
· · · · · · · · ·

The Right to Speak
and Raise Money

Having decided in the 1930s that the Fourteenth Amendment makes the First Amendment of the U.S. Constitution applicable to state and local government, the U.S. Supreme Court had to face a number of difficult questions in the 1940s. Many of these cases involved the question of what the First Amendment means by "the free exercise" of religion.

THE PLEDGE OF ALLEGIANCE

One of the most difficult issues, the question of whether or not public schools can force schoolchildren to say the Pledge of Allegiance to the American flag, came to the Court in the 1940 case of *Minersville School District v. Gobitis* (see p. 84). In this case, a group of children who were members of the Jehovah's Witnesses refused to salute the flag because they believed that their religion prohibited the worship of "graven images" and that the American flag qualified as a graven image. These children were willing to be expelled from public school rather than violate the teachings of their religion.

Eight of the nine justices agreed that these children did not have the right under the Constitution to refuse to to say the Pledge of Allegiance to the flag. In writing the majority decision, Justice Frankfurter pointed out that government had the power to force people to join the military in times of war and to require students at public colleges to take instruction in the military arts. He argued that "national unity is the basis of national security," and that being the case, surely government also had the right to force schoolchildren to say the Pledge of Allegiance to the American flag as a way of creating unity.

It is important to remember that as this decision was being written war was raging in both Europe and Asia, and many people assumed that it was only a matter of time before the United States would also be fighting for its very existence. A majority of the justices seemed to feel that it was perfectly correct for government to begin to instill in children the idea that their nation is something worth fighting and dying for.

Only one justice, Justice Stone, dissented. In his dissenting opinion, he noted that the school district rules involved in the *Gobitis* case were special. These rules were not intended to keep children from doing disloyal things or from making disloyal statements, but instead to force the children to make a statement of loyalty that they did not wish to make. Justice Stone believed that both the right of free speech and the right to freely exercise religion were involved in this case. The question was whether or not these rights, which everyone seemed to agree protected the right to speak out on issues such as government and religion, also protected the right to keep silent, the right not to speak if that speech would violate the teaching of one's religion.

Justice Stone thought that the right to speak in general, and the right to speak about religion in particular, included the right to refuse to speak. Put another way, he asked what was left of the right of free speech if government could force people to say things they did not wish to say. Not much, in his opinion. He argued that to expel children from public school because they refused to say a Pledge of Allegiance that violated their basic religious beliefs was wrong.

Justice Stone thought that the school district rules also violated the right to freely exercise religion in that they withheld a government benefit, a free public education, from one group of religions. In withholding this public benefit from those religions that refused to say the pledge, government was encouraging people to change their religious beliefs, which could be seen as also violating the Establishment Clause.

Although Justice Stone agreed with the majority of the Court that the Constitution allowed government to "suppress religious practices dangerous to morals" and to prevent religious practices that might be dangerous to "public safety, health and good order," he did not agree that refusing to pledge allegiance to the American flag fit into these categories. While he agreed that government had the power to survive in times of war, including the power to force people to perform military service and receive military training, Justice Stone did not see how forcing children to pledge allegiance to the American flag could be seen to fall into that category. What did the Pledge of Allegiance have to do with repelling invasion? He also questioned whether forcing children to say a pledge they did not believe in would actually have any positive effect on those children. He thought that the opposite was probably true, that the children would grow up to hate the country that forced them to make statements that violated their basic religious beliefs.

Justice Stone was the lone dissenter in 1940, but by 1943 major changes had taken place in the makeup of the U.S. Supreme Court. Justice Stone had been made the Chief Justice by President Roosevelt. Because the former chief justice had retired along with another justice, two new justices had joined the Court. Also, three members of the Court had thought about what Chief Justice Stone had said in his dissenting opinion in *Gobitis* and were ready to change their minds and vote with him when given the chance. That chance came with the case of *Board of Education v. Barnette* (see p. 88).

After the Supreme Court's decision in *Gobitis*, many school boards around the country began to require students to salute the flag. The West Virginia State Board of Education ordered that the flag salute become "a regular part of the program of activities in the public schools." Jehovah's Witnesses brought suit in federal court to stop enforcement of this policy. This gave the Court a chance to reconsider its *Gobitis* decision. What had been eight to one in favor of forced Pledges of Allegiance became six to three against them; *Gobitis* was overturned.

Other things had also changed in three short years. The United States was now fighting for democracy and freedom in both Europe and Asia. The standard way of saying the Pledge of Allegiance to the American flag in the 1940s involved having the children raise one arm in what we would call a "Heil Hitler"–style salute. If the current government could force little children to salute the flag in this way, could some future government force them to salute an American tyrant? The justices did not find that prospect very appealing. Also, Americans were being told they were fighting and dying to save freedom. Freedom to do what? Freedom to be forced to say things that they did not believe or that they believed violated the teachings of their religion?

The justices that voted to change the Court's collective mind argued that while government was free to force people to fight in the war if necessary, the Pledge of Allegiance was not in the same category with activities necessary to ensure the survival of the nation. They said:

> [W]ords uttered under coercion are proof of loyalty to nothing but self-interest. Love of country must spring from willing hearts and free minds, inspired by a fair administration of wise laws enacted by the people's elected representatives within the bounds of express constitutional prohibitions.

These justices could not see how the war effort depended on forcing "little children to participate in a ceremony which ends in nothing for them but a fear of spiritual condemnation."

Justice Murphy wrote a concurring opinion, in which he argued that forcing people to speak against their will violated their freedom to believe as they wished, and that everyone agreed that the right to freely exercise religion protected the right to believe. Trying to force people to say things they did not believe, he argued, amounted to trying to force people to believe something that the state wanted them to believe, and that clearly was beyond the power of the state under the First Amendment.

Justice Frankfurter, who wrote the majority decision in *Gobitis*, wrote the dissenting opinion in *Barnette*. He argued that because this is a complex area, the Court should defer to legislatures and school boards. President Roosevelt had appointed the members of the Supreme Court to bring an end to the days when the members of the Court believed they could second-guess Congress and state legislatures on every issue.

While a majority of the justices agreed with Justice Frankfurter in principle, they also believed that the rights of free speech and free exercise of religion had to take precedence in this case if the First Amendment was to amount to more than empty words on a piece of paper.

SOLICITATION OF MONEY FOR RELIGIOUS PURPOSES

The Supreme Court handed down several related decisions from 1940 to 1953, all of which involved Jehovah's Witnesses and the question of just how far the right to freely exercise religion went. The 1940 case of *Cantwell v. Connecticut* involved Newton Cantwell and his two sons, all Jehovah's Witnesses. They were convicted of violating a law that made it illegal to solicit money for religious purposes from anyone other than members of your own religion without a certificate from the government. A unanimous Supreme Court found this law to be a violation of the Free Exercise Clause of the First Amendment.

The justices thought that the right to freely exercise religion included, at a minimum, the right to preach and speak to others about those religious beliefs. This right to speak and preach included the right to ask for money to support spreading a particular religious belief. While it was one thing for government to attempt to control door-to-door solicitors, it could not single out people who were soliciting in the name of religion and apply special regulations to them.

This rule also had the effect of discriminating against newer religions, which unlike most established religions would not be able to raise enough money from their members alone. In other words, not only did this rule discriminate against the religious, but it also put a burden on only some religious sects. This made the law unconstitutional as a violation of the Establishment Clause as well.

A similar case in 1943 was much more difficult for the Court to decide (*Martin v. Struthers*). Ms. Martin, a Jehovah's Witness, had been convicted of violating a city ordinance in Struthers, Ohio, that made it illegal for anyone to distribute "handbills, circulars or advertisements" by means of ringing doorbells or "otherwise summoning the residents to the door." This was different from the law in the *Cantwell* case. In *Cantwell*, only religious solicitors were affected by the rule. In *Martin*, all solicitors were affected, regardless of the reason they wanted to "summon the residents" to the door. Solicitors could still distribute literature door-to-door, but they could not ring doorbells or knock at the door. What was the reason for this ordinance? Many of the people who lived in Struthers, Ohio, worked the night shift, so they were trying to sleep during the day. The city was trying to make this easier by sparing these people the noise and disturbance that comes from door-to-door solicitation.

Five justices thought that this law violated both the right of free speech and the right to freely exercise religion by "propagating the faith." Going door-to-door to talk to people was one of the few ways a new sect could reach out for converts. The Jehovah's Witnesses considered door-to-door solicitation to be their main way of adding people to their fold. If they could not summon people to the door, they would be deprived of their major means of spreading their religious beliefs. Of course, under this law they were allowed to leave something quietly at the door, but a majority of the justices accepted the argument of the Jehovah's Witnesses that this was not nearly as effective as actually talking to someone face-to-face.

The city argued that ringing doorbells was a nuisance, and that in some instances those going door-to-door were simply criminals trying to find out if anyone was home. A majority of the justices did not feel that these potential problems outweighed the right of people in general to use this method to communicate with their fellow citizens and the right of the religious to spread their message in this particular way. Again, the issue could be raised that established religious groups with lots of money could use other means to communicate, but newer and poorer groups could not afford to buy advertising space in newspapers or on the radio and would be effectively silenced if they could not go door-to-door.

Justice Frankfurter wrote a dissenting opinion, which was joined by three other justices. These four justices argued that the people living in Struthers, Ohio, had a right to be left alone on their private property and a right to be free from unwanted noise while they tried to sleep in preparation for another night's work.

A majority of the members of the Court essentially said that there is a price to be paid by a society that dedicates itself to the rights protected by the First Amendment. Being awakened once in a while by a Jehovah's Witness or by the members of some other religious sect that believes going door-to-door is a useful strategy is one of the prices Americans pay for freedom. In 1943 a majority of the Court could say that if millions of American soldiers could fight and die for freedom in Europe and Asia, then the citizens of Struthers, Ohio, could suffer a little inconvenience once in a while for the same cause.

LICENSE FEES

In 1942 and 1943 the Court handed down a decision and again changed its mind. In 1942 five justices ruled that the city of Opelika, Alabama, could require anyone selling books, even Jehovah's Witnesses, to obtain a license and pay a fee (*Jones v. Opelika*). The Court majority thought that because the license and fee requirement applied to everyone, it was not a particular hardship on the religious. Rather, the Court viewed the requirement as an attempt to control a commercial activity and raise money.

In 1943, however, one member of the Court had been replaced, and what had been five to four in favor of the license fee became five to four against it (*Murdock v. Pennsylvania*). The city of Jeannette, Pennsylvania, had imposed a flat fee on anyone wishing to sell door-to-door. The more days on which the salespeople wished to sell, the higher the license fee. The fee for one day was $1.50; for a week, $7.00; and for three weeks, $20.00. The Jehovah's Witnesses, who were selling books for 25 cents and 5 cents each, would often sell less than $1.50 worth of books in one day.

Justice Douglas believed that, given these facts, even a small fee, when applied to people selling religious literature, was too much. Such people often have little or no money; if they have to pay a flat fee regardless of whether or not they actually make sales, then they may be discouraged from this kind of activity. If Struthers, Ohio, could not outlaw door-to-door selling altogether (*Martin v. Struthers*), then Jeannette, Pennsylvania, would not be allowed to accomplish the same thing by imposing a flat license fee. A sales tax that would be paid only if something were actually sold and would not unduly interfere with the activity of going door-to-door to sell religious literature would be permissible, in Justice Douglas's opinion. He noted that the power to tax an activity at a flat rate, regardless of the amount of money that activity raised, was the power to prevent the activity altogether.

CHILD LABOR LAWS

In 1944 the Court had to decide whether or not the state of Massachusetts could prevent a nine-year-old girl from selling copies of the "Watchtower," a publication of the Jehovah's Witnesses (*Prince v. Massachusetts*). Sarah Prince took her nine-year-old ward with her when she went out selling the "Watchtower" and allowed the little girl to sell some copies herself. Massachusetts argued that this practice violated its child labor laws. While the little girl was free to pass out literature, the law did not allow her to sell things on the street at that age, even religious material.

Five of the justices agreed that Massachusetts had the power to regulate child labor, and that the state could prevent this kind of religious work from being performed by underage children. While Sarah Prince argued that a distinction should be drawn between this kind of religious work and other types of work, the Court majority did not wish to get involved in trying to draw such a line. Where would the line go? Was selling religious literature acceptable but building churches unacceptable?

The four dissenting justices did not feel the child labor laws should reach this kind of activity. The purpose of child labor laws is to make sure children attend school and are not exposed to danger. The dissenters could not see how selling the "Watchtower" exposed the little girl to any danger she would not otherwise face standing on a street corner, and the work did not prevent her from attending school.

BALANCING RELIGIOUS FREEDOM AND THE RIGHTS OF OTHERS

In 1946 the case of *Marsh v. Alabama* came before the court. A Jehovah's Witness had been convicted of trespassing on private property. The property was an entire town that was owned by the Gulf Shipbuilding Company; the company had posted "private property" and "no solicitation without written permission" signs at the borders of the town. The Jehovah's Witness entered the town to pass out religious literature without following company procedure, and the company called the police to have the Jehovah's Witness arrested for trespassing.

In previous cases the Court had ruled that a town could control the passing out of literature with reasonable regulations but could not prevent this activity altogether. A majority of the justices thought that the same rule should apply in this case, even though the entire town was technically private property. After all, while a technical trespass had been committed, no one had broken into a building or destroyed property. A Jehovah's Witness had simply stood on a street corner passing out literature, as he had done in dozens of towns before.

Three justices dissented, arguing that the right of private property should take precedence over the right of free speech and the right to freely exercise religion. They believed that homeowners should be free to keep people out of their homes, and companies should have the same right. Again, in the battle between property rights on the one hand and free speech and free exercise of religion rights on the other, the rights to speak and to exercise religion were found to be supreme.

In 1953 a unanimous Court overturned the conviction of a Jehovah's Witness who had given a religious address in a public park in Pawtucket, Rhode Island (*Fowler v. Rhode Island*). The case was easy for the Court to decide because the city had allowed other religious groups to hold religious services in the park in the past. Because of that, the city would not be allowed to discriminate against Jehovah's Witnesses.

In 1992 the Court reaffirmed these decisions in the case of *Krishna v. Lee*. Members of the Krishna religion wanted to solicit money and pass out literature at the airports in and around New York City. A majority of the justices ruled that the airports could prevent the Krishnas from asking for money inside the airports. These justices thought that because people would have to stop and get out their wallets in order to respond to this request, this kind of activity would be too disruptive and would unreasonably interfere with the flow of people and baggage through these busy airports.

On the other hand, a majority of the justices believed that simply passing out literature would not be nearly as disruptive, and that the Krishnas had to be allowed to do that. The airports could restrict this activity to areas such as the lobby, however, to minimize the disruption. The airports could control the area where religious literature could be distributed, but they could not prevent its distribution completely.

CONCLUSION

Over the course of half a century, the U.S. Supreme Court has tried to strike a reasonable balance between the rights of the religious to speak out, solicit funds, and sell religious literature on the one hand, and the rights of other citizens to not be bothered in places like parks and airports. Generally the Court has tried to recognize the reality of each situation. Someone sitting in an airport lobby or in their living room is not really bothered by being asked to accept a piece of religious literature; whereas someone rushing to catch a flight is bothered by being asked for money. It is not reasonable for cities to prevent door-to-door solicitation by the religious, but it is reasonable to prevent child labor, regardless of the nature of the work involved. Also, cities should not be able to accomplish with a large license fee what they cannot accomplish with an outright ban.

While it is not always clear what the right to freely exercise religion includes, in these decisions the Court has tried to make it clear that this right at least includes the right to think and speak about religion, and also includes the right to pass out literature and solicit contributions within reasonable limits. Laws that place too great a limitation on these activities, such as laws prohibiting door-to-door solicitation, are unconstitutional. The right to freely exercise religion also includes the right to sell books free of unreasonable regulations and taxes. Free exercise of religion also includes an individual's right to refuse to say things that he or she does not wish to say, even a schoolchild's right to refuse to say the Pledge of Allegiance to the American flag.

CASE DECISIONS

In *Minersville School District v. Gobitis* and *Board of Education v. Barnette*, the Court had to determine whether or not a public school can expel children who refuse to salute the American flag because they believe it violates their religion. These two cases exhibit a major shift in the thinking of the Supreme Court over a very short period of time. The *Minersville School District v. Gobitis* decision was handed down in 1940. All but one justice agreed that a school district could expel children who refused to salute the American flag without violating the First Amendment of the U.S. Constitution. Justice Frankfurter wrote the opinion for the eight-member majority, and Justice Stone wrote the only dissenting opinion. Both opinions are included here.

Three years later, with *Board of Education v. Barnette*, two justices had been replaced and three had changed their minds. This made six justices who believed that forcing children to say the Pledge of Allegiance to the American flag on pain of expulsion from public school did violate the First Amendment. Justice Jackson wrote the opinion for the majority, while Justices Black, Douglas, and Murphy wrote short concurring opinions, all of which are included here. Justice Frankfurter wrote a dissenting opinion, which is not included.

Following are excerpts from the case decisions.

* * * * * * * * * *

MINERSVILLE SCHOOL DISTRICT v. GOBITIS
310 U.S. 586 (1940)

MR. JUSTICE FRANKFURTER delivered the opinion of the Court.

A grave responsibility confronts this Court whenever in course of litigation it must reconcile the conflicting claims of liberty and authority. But when the liberty invoked is liberty of conscience, and the authority is authority to safeguard the nation's fellowship, judicial conscience is put to its severest test. Of such a nature is the present controversy.

Lillian Gobitis, aged twelve, and her brother William, aged ten, were expelled from the public schools of Minersville, Pennsylvania, for refusing to salute the national flag as part of a daily school exercise. The local Board of Education required both teachers and pupils to participate in this ceremony. The ceremony is a familiar one. The right hand is placed on the breast and the following pledge recited in unison: "I pledge allegiance to my flag, and to the Republic for which it stands; one nation indivisible, with liberty and justice for all." While the words are spoken, teachers and pupils extend their right hands in salute to the flag. The Gobitis family are affiliated with "Jehovah's Witnesses," for whom the Bible as the Word of God is the supreme authority. The children had been brought up conscientiously to believe that such a gesture of respect for the flag was forbidden by command of Scripture. . . .

The religious liberty which the Constitution protects has never excluded legislation of general scope not directed against doctrinal loyalties of particular sects. Judicial nullification of legislation cannot be justified by attributing to the framers of the Bill of Rights views for which there is no historic warrant. Conscientious scruples have not, in the course of the long struggle for religious toleration, relieved the individual from obedience to a general law not aimed at the promotion or restriction of religious beliefs. The mere possession of religious convictions which contradict the relevant concerns of a political society does not relieve the citizen from the discharge of political responsibilities. The necessity for this adjustment has again and again been recognized. In a number of situations the exertion of political authority has been sustained, while basic considerations of religious freedom have been left inviolate. *Reynolds v. United States*, 98 U.S. 145; *Davis v. Beason*, 133 U.S. 333; *Selective Draft Law Cases*, 245 U.S. 366; *Hamilton v. Regents*, 293 U.S. 245. In all these cases the general laws in question, upheld in their application to those who refused obedience from religious conviction, were manifestations of specific powers of government deemed by the legislature essential to secure and maintain that orderly, tranquil, and free society without which religious toleration itself is unattainable. Nor does the freedom of speech assured by Due Process move in a more absolute circle of immunity than that enjoyed by religious freedom. Even if it were assumed that freedom of speech goes beyond the historic concept of full opportunity to utter and to disseminate views, however heretical or offensive to dominant opinion, and includes freedom from conveying what may be deemed an implied but rejected affirmation, the question remains whether school children, like the Gobitis children, must be excused from conduct required of all the other children in the promotion of national cohesion. We are dealing with an interest inferior to none in the hierarchy of legal values. National unity is the basis of national security. To deny the legislature the right to select appropriate means for its attainment presents a totally different order of problem from that of the propriety of subordinating the possible ugliness of littered streets to the free expression of opinion through distribution of handbills. . . .

The preciousness of the family relation, the authority and independence which give dignity to parenthood, indeed the enjoyment of all freedom, presuppose the kind of ordered society which is summarized by our flag. A society which is dedicated to the preservation of these ultimate values of civilization may in self-protection utilize the educational process for inculcating those almost unconscious feelings which bind men together in a comprehending loyalty, whatever may be their lesser differences and difficulties. That is to say, the process may be utilized so long as men's right to believe as they please, to win others to their way of belief, and their right to assemble in their chosen places of worship for the devotional ceremonies of their faith, are all fully respected.

Judicial review, itself a limitation on popular government, is a fundamental part of our constitutional scheme. But to the legislature no less than to courts is committed the guardianship of deeply-cherished liberties. See *Missouri, K. & T. Ry. Co. v. May*, 194 U.S. 267, 270. Where all the effective means of inducing political changes are left free from interference, education in the abandonment of foolish legislation is itself a training in liberty. To fight out the wise use of legislative authority in the forum of public opinion and before legislative assemblies rather than to transfer such a contest to the judicial arena, serves to vindicate the self-confidence of a free people.

Reversed.

Dissenting Opinion   MR. JUSTICE STONE, dissenting:

I think the judgment below should be affirmed.

Two youths, now fifteen and sixteen years of age, are by the judgment of this Court held liable to expulsion from the public schools and to denial of all publicly supported educational privileges because of their refusal to yield to the compulsion of a law which commands their participation in a school ceremony contrary to their religious convictions. They and their father are citizens and have not exhibited by any action or statement of opinion, any disloyalty to the Government of the United States. They are ready and willing to obey all its laws which do not conflict with what they sincerely believe to be the higher commandments of God. It is not doubted that these convictions are religious, that they are genuine, or that the refusal to yield to the compulsion of the law is in good faith and with all sincerity. It would be a denial of their faith as well as the teachings of most religions to say that children of their age could not have religious convictions.

The law which is thus sustained is unique in the history of Anglo-American legislation. It does more than suppress freedom of speech and more than prohibit the free exercise of religion, which concededly are forbidden by the First Amendment and are violations of the liberty guaranteed by the Fourteenth. For by this law the state seeks to coerce these children to express a sentiment which, as they interpret it, they do not entertain, and which violates their deepest religious convictions. It is not denied that such compulsion is a prohibited infringement of personal liberty, freedom of speech and religion, guaranteed by the Bill of Rights, except in so far as it may be justified and supported as a proper exercise of the state's power over public education. Since the state, in competition with parents, may through teaching in the public schools indoctrinate the minds of the young, it is said that in aid of its undertaking to inspire loyalty and devotion to constituted authority and the flag which symbolizes it, it may coerce the pupil to make affirmation contrary to his belief and in violation of his religious faith. And, finally, it is said that since the Minersville School Board and others are of the opinion that the country will be better served by conformity than by the observance of religious liberty which the Constitution prescribes, the courts are not free to pass judgment on the Board's choice.

Concededly the constitutional guaranties of personal liberty are not always absolutes. Government has a right to survive and powers conferred upon it are not necessarily set at naught by the express prohibitions of the Bill of Rights. It may make war and raise armies. To that end it may compel citizens to give military service, *Selective Draft Law Cases*, 245 U.S. 366, and subject them to military training despite their religious objections. *Hamilton v. Regents*, 293 U.S. 245. It may suppress religious practices dangerous to morals, and presumably those also which are inimical to public safety, health and good order.*Davis v. Beason*, 133 U.S. 333. But it is a long step, and one which I am unable to take, to the position that government may, as a supposed educational measure and as a means of disciplining the young, compel public affirmations which violate their religious conscience.

The very fact that we have constitutional guaranties of civil liberties and the specificity of their command where freedom of speech and of religion are concerned require some accommodation of the powers which government normally exercises, when no question of civil liberty is involved, to the constitutional demand that those liberties be protected against the action of government itself. The state concededly has power to require and control the education of its citizens, but it cannot by a general law compelling attendance at public schools preclude attendance at a private school adequate in its instruction, where the parent seeks to secure for the child the benefits of religious instruction not provided by the public school. *Pierce v. Society of*

Sisters, 268 U.S. 510. And only recently we have held that the state's authority to control its public streets by generally applicable regulations is not an absolute to which free speech must yield, and cannot be made the medium of its suppression, *Hague v. Committee for Industrial Organization*, 307 U.S. 496, 514, *et seq.*, any more than can its authority to penalize littering of the streets by a general law be used to suppress the distribution of handbills as a means of communicating ideas to their recipients. *Schneider v. State*, 308 U.S. 147. . . .

The guaranties of civil liberty are but guaranties of freedom of the human mind and spirit and of reasonable freedom and opportunity to express them. They presuppose the right of the individual to hold such opinions as he will and to give them reasonably free expression, and his freedom, and that of the state as well, to teach and persuade others by the communication of ideas. The very essence of the liberty which they guaranty is the freedom of the individual from compulsion as to what he shall think and what he shall say, at least where the compulsion is to bear false witness to his religion. If these guaranties are to have any meaning they must, I think, be deemed to withhold from the state any authority to compel belief or the expression of it where that expression violates religious convictions, whatever may be the legislative view of the desirability of such compulsion. . . .

The Constitution expresses more than the conviction of the people that democratic processes must be preserved at all costs. It is also an expression of faith and a command that freedom of mind and spirit must be preserved, which government must obey, if it is to adhere to that justice and moderation without which no free government can exist. For this reason it would seem that legislation which operates to repress the religious freedom of small minorities, which is admittedly within the scope of the protection of the Bill of Rights, must at least be subject to the same judicial scrutiny as legislation which we have recently held to infringe the constitutional liberty of religious and racial minorities.

With such scrutiny I cannot say that the inconveniences which may attend some sensible adjustment of school discipline in order that the religious convictions of these children may be spared, presents a problem so momentous or pressing as to outweigh the freedom from compulsory violation of religious faith which has been thought worthy of constitutional protection.

BOARD OF EDUCATION v. BARNETTE
319 U.S. 624 (1943)

MR. JUSTICE JACKSON delivered the opinion of the Court.

Following the decision by this Court on June 3, 1940, in *Minersville School District v. Gobitis*, 310 U.S. 586, the West Virginia legislature amended its statutes to require all schools therein to conduct courses of instruction in history, civics, and in the Constitutions of the United States and of the State "for the purpose of teaching, fostering and perpetuating the ideals, principles and spirit of Americanism, and increasing the knowledge of the organization and machinery of the government." Appellant Board of Education was directed, with advice of the State Superintendent of Schools, to "prescribe the courses of study covering these subjects" for public schools. The Act made it the duty of private, parochial and denominational schools to prescribe courses of study "similar to those required for the public schools."

The Board of Education on January 9, 1942, adopted a resolution containing recitals taken largely from the Court's *Gobitis* opinion and ordering that the salute to the flag become "a regular part of the program of activities in the public schools," that all teachers and pupils "shall be required to participate in the salute honoring the Nation represented by the Flag; provided, however, that refusal to salute the Flag be regarded as an act of insubordination, and shall be dealt with accordingly." . . .

Appellees, citizens of the United States and of West Virginia, brought suit in the United States District Court for themselves and others similarly situated asking its injunction to restrain enforcement of these laws and regulations against Jehovah's Witnesses. The Witnesses are an unincorporated body teaching that the obligation imposed by law of God is superior to that of laws enacted by temporal government. Their religious beliefs include a literal version of Exodus, Chapter 20, verses 4 and 5, which says: "Thou shalt not make unto thee any graven image, or any likeness of anything that is in heaven above, or that is in the earth beneath, or that is in the water under the earth; thou shalt not bow down thyself to them nor serve them." They consider that the flag is an "image" within this command. For this reason they refuse to salute it. . . .

As the present Chief Justice said in dissent in the *Gobitis* case, the State may "require teaching by instruction and study of all in our history and in the structure and organization of our government, including the guaranties of civil liberty, which tend to inspire patriotism and love of country." 310 U.S. at 604. Here, however, we are dealing with a compulsion of students to declare a belief. They are not merely made acquainted with the flag salute so that they may be informed as to what it is or even what it means. The issue here is whether this slow and easily neglected route to aroused loyalties constitutionally may be short-cut by substituting a compulsory salute and slogan. This issue is not prejudiced by the Court's previous holding that where a State, without compelling attendance, extends college facilities to pupils who voluntarily enroll, it may prescribe military training as part of the course without offense to the Constitution. It was held that those who take advantage of its opportunities may not on ground of conscience refuse compliance with such conditions. *Hamilton v. Regents*, 293 U.S. 245. In the present case attendance is not optional. That case is also to be distinguished from the present one because, independently of college privileges or requirements, the State has power to raise militia and impose the duties of service therein upon its citizens. . . .

The *Gobitis* decision, however, *assumed*, as did the argument in that case and in this, that power exists in the State to impose the flag salute discipline upon school children in general. The Court only examined and rejected a claim based on religious beliefs of immunity from an unquestioned general rule. The question which underlies the flag salute controversy is whether such a ceremony so touching matters of opinion and political attitude may be imposed upon the individual by official authority under powers committed to any political organization under our Constitution. We examine rather than assume existence of this power and, against this broader definition of issues in this case, reëxamine specific grounds assigned for the *Gobitis* decision.

1. It was said that the flag-salute controversy confronted the Court with "the problem which Lincoln cast in memorable dilemma: 'Must a government of necessity be too *strong* for the liberties of its people, or too *weak* to maintain its own existence?' " and that the answer must be in favor of strength. *Minersville School District v. Gobitis, supra*, at 596.

We think these issues may be examined free of pressure or restraint growing out of such considerations.

It may be doubted whether Mr. Lincoln would have thought that the strength of government to maintain itself would be impressively vindicated by our confirming power of the State to expel a handful of children from school. Such oversimplification, so handy in political debate, often lacks the precision necessary to postulates of judicial reasoning. If validly applied to this problem, the utterance cited would resolve every issue of power in favor of those in authority and would require us to override every liberty thought to weaken or delay execution of their policies.

Government of limited power need not be anemic government. Assurance that rights are secure tends to diminish fear and jealousy of strong government, and by making us feel safe to live under it makes for its better support. Without promise of a limiting Bill of Rights it is doubtful if our Constitution could have mustered enough strength to enable its ratification. To enforce those rights today is not to choose weak government over strong government. It is only to adhere as a means of strength to individual freedom of mind in preference to officially disciplined uniformity for which history indicates a disappointing and disastrous end.

The subject now before us exemplifies this principle. Free public education, if faithful to the ideal of secular instruction and political neutrality, will not be partisan or enemy of any class, creed, party, or faction. If it is to impose any ideological discipline, however, each party or denomination must seek to control, or failing that, to weaken the influence of the educational system. Observance of the limitations of the Constitution will not weaken government in the field appropriate for its exercise.

2. It was also considered in the *Gobitis* case that functions of educational officers in States, counties and school districts were such that to interfere with their authority "would in effect make us the school board for the country." *Id.* at 598.

The Fourteenth Amendment, as now applied to the States, protects the citizen against the State itself and all of its creatures—Boards of Education not excepted. These have, of course, important, delicate, and highly discretionary functions, but none that they may not perform within the limits of the Bill of Rights. That they are educating the young for citizenship is reason for scrupulous protection of Constitutional freedoms of the individual, if we are not to strangle the free mind at its source and teach youth to discount important principles of our government as mere platitudes.

Such Boards are numerous and their territorial jurisdiction often small. But small and local authority may feel less sense of responsibility to the Constitution, and agencies of publicity may be less vigilant in calling it to account. The action of Congress in making flag observance voluntary and respecting the conscience of the objector in a matter so vital as raising the Army contrasts sharply with these local regulations in matters relatively trivial to the welfare of the nation. There are village tyrants as well as village Hampdens, but none who acts under color of law is beyond reach of the Constitution.

3. The *Gobitis* opinion reasoned that this is a field "where courts possess no marked and certainly no controlling competence," that it is committed to the legislatures as well as the courts to guard cherished liberties and that it is constitutionally appropriate to "fight out the wise use of legislative authority in the forum of public opinion and before legislative assemblies rather than to transfer such a contest to the judicial arena," since all the "effective means of inducing political changes are left free." *Id.* at 597–598, 600.

The very purpose of a Bill of Rights was to withdraw certain subjects from the vicissitudes of political controversy, to place them beyond the reach of majorities and officials and to establish them as legal principles to be applied by the courts. One's right to life, liberty, and property, to free speech, a free press, freedom of worship and assembly, and other fundamental rights may not be submitted to vote; they depend on the outcome of no elections. . . .

4. Lastly, and this is the very heart of the *Gobitis* opinion, it reasons that "National unity is the basis of national security," that the authorities have "the right to select appropriate means for its attainment," and hence reaches the conclusion that such compulsory measures toward "national unity" are constitutional. *Id.* at 595. Upon the verity of this assumption depends our answer in this case.

National unity as an end which officials may foster by persuasion and example is not in question. The problem is whether under our Constitution compulsion as here employed is a permissible means for its achievement.

Struggles to coerce uniformity of sentiment in support of some end thought essential to their time and country have been waged by many good as well as by evil men. Nationalism is a relatively recent phenomenon but at other times and places the ends have been racial or territorial security, support of a dynasty or regime, and particular plans for saving souls. As first and moderate methods to attain unity have failed, those bent on its accomplishment must resort to an ever-increasing severity. As governmental pressure toward unity becomes greater, so strife becomes more bitter as to whose unity it shall be. Probably no deeper division of our people could proceed from any provocation than from finding it necessary to choose what doctrine and whose program public educational officials shall compel youth to unite in embracing. Ultimate futility of such attempts to compel coherence is the lesson of every such effort from the Roman drive to stamp out Christianity as a disturber of its pagan unity, the Inquisition, as a means to religious and dynastic unity, the Siberian exiles as a means to Russian unity, down to the fast failing efforts of our present totalitarian enemies. Those who begin coercive elimination of dissent soon find themselves exterminating dissenters. Compulsory unification of opinion achieves only the unanimity of the graveyard.

It seems trite but necessary to say that the First Amendment to our Constitution was designed to avoid these ends by avoiding these beginnings. There is no mysticism in the American concept of the State or of the nature or origin of its authority. We set up government by consent of the governed, and the Bill of Rights denies those in power any legal opportunity to coerce that consent. Authority here is to be controlled by public opinion, not public opinion by authority.

The case is made difficult not because the principles of its decision are obscure but because the flag involved is our own. Nevertheless, we apply the limitations of the Constitution with no fear that freedom to be intellectually and spiritually diverse or even contrary will disintegrate the social organization. To believe that patriotism will not flourish if patriotic ceremonies are voluntary and spontaneous instead of a compulsory routine is to make an unflattering estimate of the appeal of our institutions to free minds. We can have intellectual individualism and the rich cultural diversities that we owe to exceptional minds only at the price of occasional eccentricity and abnormal attitudes. When they are so harmless to others or to the State as those we deal with here, the price is not too great. But freedom to differ is not limited to things that do not matter much. That would be a mere shadow of freedom. The test of its substance is the right to differ as to things that touch the heart of the existing order.

If there is any fixed star in our constitutional constellation, it is that no official, high or petty, can prescribe what shall be orthodox in politics, nationalism, religion, or other matters of opinion or force citizens to confess by word or act their faith therein. If there are any circumstances which permit an exception, they do not now occur to us.

We think the action of the local authorities in compelling the flag salute and pledge transcends constitutional limitations on their power and invades the sphere of intellect and spirit which it is the purpose of the First Amendment to our Constitution to reserve from all official control.

The decision of this Court in *Minersville School District v. Gobitis* and the holdings of those few *per curiam* decisions which preceded and foreshadowed it are overruled, and the judgment enjoining enforcement of the West Virginia Regulation is

Affirmed.

Concurring Opinion   MR. JUSTICE BLACK and MR. JUSTICE DOUGLAS, concurring:

We are substantially in agreement with the opinion just read, but since we originally joined with the Court in the *Gobitis* case, it is appropriate that we make a brief statement of reasons for our change of view.

Reluctance to make the Federal Constitution a rigid bar against state regulation of conduct thought inimical to the public welfare was the controlling influence which moved us to consent to the *Gobitis* decision. Long reflection convinced us that although the principle is sound, its application in the particular case was wrong. . . . We believe that the statute before us fails to accord full scope to the freedom of religion secured to the appellees by the First and Fourteenth Amendments.

The statute requires the appellees to participate in a ceremony aimed at inculcating respect for the flag and for this country. The Jehovah's Witnesses, without any desire to show disrespect for either the flag or the country, interpret the Bible as commanding, at the risk of God's displeasure, that they not go through the form of a pledge of allegiance to any flag. The devoutness of their belief is evidenced by their willingness to suffer persecution and punishment, rather than make the pledge.

No well-ordered society can leave to the individuals an absolute right to make final decisions, unassailable by the State, as to everything they will or will not do. The First Amendment does not go so far. Religious faiths, honestly held, do not free individuals from responsibility to conduct themselves obediently to laws which are either imperatively necessary to protect society as a whole from grave and pressingly imminent dangers or which, without any general prohibition, merely regulate time, place or manner of religious activity. Decision as to the constitutionality of particular laws which strike at the substance of religious tenets and practices must be made by this Court. The duty is a solemn one, and in meeting it we cannot say that a failure, because of religious scruples, to assume a particular physical position and to repeat the words of a patriotic formula creates a grave danger to the nation. Such a statutory exaction is a form of test oath, and the test oath has always been abhorrent in the United States.

Words uttered under coercion are proof of loyalty to nothing but self-interest. Love of country must spring from willing hearts and free minds, inspired by a fair administration of wise laws enacted by the people's elected representatives within the bounds of express constitutional prohibitions. These laws must, to be consistent with the First Amendment, permit the widest toleration of conflicting viewpoints consistent with a society of free men.

Neither our domestic tranquillity in peace nor our martial effort in war depend on compelling little children to participate in a ceremony which ends in nothing for them but a fear of spiritual condemnation. If, as we think, their fears are groundless, time and reason are the proper antidotes for their errors. The ceremonial, when enforced against conscientious objectors, more likely to defeat than to serve its high purpose, is a handy implement for disguised religious persecution. As such, it is inconsistent with our Constitution's plan and purpose.

Concurring Opinion   MR. JUSTICE MURPHY, concurring:

I agree with the opinion of the Court and join in it. . . .

The right of freedom of thought and of religion as guaranteed by the Constitution against State action includes both the right to speak freely and the right to refrain from speaking at all, except insofar as essential operations of government may require it for the preservation of an orderly society—as in the case of compulsion to give evidence in court. Without wishing to disparage the purposes and intentions of those who hope to inculcate sentiments of loyalty and patriotism by requiring a declaration of allegiance as a feature of public education, or unduly belittle the benefits that may accrue therefrom, I am impelled to conclude that such a requirement is not essential to the maintenance of effective government and orderly society. To many it is deeply distasteful to join in a public chorus of affirmation of private belief. By some, including the members of this sect, it is apparently regarded as incompatible with a primary religious obligation and therefore a restriction on religious freedom. Official compulsion to affirm what is contrary to one's religious beliefs is the antithesis of freedom of worship which, it is well to recall, was achieved in this country only after what Jefferson characterized as the "severest contests in which I have ever been engaged."

I am unable to agree that the benefits that may accrue to society from the compulsory flag salute are sufficiently definite and tangible to justify the invasion of freedom and privacy that is entailed or to compensate for a restraint on the freedom of the individual to be vocal or silent according to his conscience or personal inclination. The trenchant words in the preamble to the Virginia Statute for Religious Freedom remain unanswerable: ". . . all attempts to influence [the mind] by temporal punishments, or burdens, or by civil incapacitations, tend only to beget habits of hypocrisy and meanness, . . ." Any spark of love for country which may be generated in a child or his associates by forcing him to make what is to him an empty gesture and recite words wrung from him contrary to his religious beliefs is overshadowed by the desirability of preserving freedom of conscience to the full. It is in that freedom and the example of persuasion, not in force and compulsion, that the real unity of America lies.

·····················DISCUSSION QUESTIONS·····················

1. In *Board of Education v. Barnette*, the U.S. Supreme Court decided that children could not be forced to say the Pledge of Allegiance to the flag. The Court based this decision in part on the right of free exercise of religion and in part on the right of free speech. Could you argue that a child who does not think that the flag is a "graven image" and whose religion is not offended by the pledge should also be allowed to refuse to take part in this ceremony?

2. If government may not prevent solicitation of funds by the religious, may it stop the same activity by atheists?

3. The Court has ruled that solicitation of money in a busy airport is something government can prevent because it is too disruptive. What other activities do you think the government could prevent because they are too disruptive?

4. If the government cannot force schoolchildren to say the Pledge of Allegiance to the flag, is there anything the government can force people to say? If so, what kinds of forced speech do you think would be legal?

CHAPTER
six
•••••••••

Education, Conscience, and Religion

Before the 1920s, the U.S. Supreme Court interpreted the Fourteenth Amendment as protecting liberties, but was not very specific concerning what these liberties were. In the 1920s the Court had to face two decisions that helped to define which liberties were protected. Both cases involved the right to receive an education.

THE RIGHT TO RECEIVE AN EDUCATION

The 1923 case of *Meyer v. Nebraska* involved laws, which had been passed in a number of states during and soon after World War I, that made it illegal to teach the German language to children below a specific age. The Nebraska law made it illegal to teach German or any other modern language before the ninth grade. Mr. Meyer was convicted of teaching German to 10-year-old children who were attending a private school, the Zion Parochial School, and he appealed his conviction under Nebraska law to the U.S. Supreme Court.

The question before the Court was whether or not one of the "liberties" protected by the Fourteenth Amendment was the liberty to learn. Does the Fourteenth Amendment guarantee to people the right to study subjects such as the modern foreign languages? The Court said that it did. Justice McReynolds, writing for the Court, responded to Nebraska's argument that children should learn English before they attempt to learn other languages by saying:

> That the State may do much, go very far, indeed, in order to improve the quality of its citizens, physically, mentally and morally, is clear; but the individual has certain fundamental rights which must be respected. The protection of the Constitution extends to all, to those who speak other

languages as well as to those born with English on the tongue. Perhaps it would be highly advantageous if all had ready understanding of our ordinary speech, but this cannot be coerced by methods which conflict with the Constitution—a desirable end cannot be promoted by prohibited means.

He went on to say that while the Court had not been very specific about what "liberties" the Fourteenth Amendment protected, these liberties certainly included the right to "acquire useful knowledge."

Two justices dissented in Meyer, arguing that states should be free to control the curriculum of both public and private schools as long as state restrictions were reasonable. These two justices thought that it was not unreasonable to require students to master English during their early years in school.

Two years later, in 1925, the Court faced a related question (*Pierce v. Society of Sisters* [see p. 104]). The state of Oregon had held a referendum to change its constitution. A majority of the citizens had voted to place in the Oregon constitution the requirement that all children attend only public school. A number of private schools appealed this new provision to the U.S. Supreme Court, but the new law was particularly harmful to the Society of Sisters, which had been running Catholic schools in Oregon since 1890. The question in this case was whether the Fourteenth Amendment protected the right of students to attend private schools. The Court answered that it did. There were no dissenters in the *Society of Sisters* case. All of the justices agreed that the Fourteenth Amendment protected the right of parents to send their children to private school.

The Court acknowledged that the state had the right to control all schools, even private religious schools, to ensure that the teachers were of "good moral character" and that "certain studies plainly essential to good citizenship" were taught. States could also prevent the teaching of anything that would be harmful to the "public welfare." The Court concluded that while the state could regulate private schools, it could not outlaw them altogether.

These two decisions, handed down in the 1920s, stand for the proposition that people in the United States, even schoolchildren, have a right to seek out knowledge, as long as that knowledge is not obviously harmful to the public welfare, and they have the right to attend private schools whether the schools are religious or not. In both of these cases the people affected attended private religious schools, but the Supreme Court justices did not come to their conclusions on the basis of the right to freely exercise religion. These decisions were based on the much broader principle that everyone, regardless of religion, has a right to learn and to seek out knowledge. Today we might view this as an aspect of the right of free speech; part of the right of free speech is the right to teach and the right to learn, and the flip side of the right of free speech is the right to hear and to be educated so that citizens can take full of advantage of what they hear and be most effective in what they say.

If the Court had based this right to receive a private education on the right to freely exercise religion, then it could have been argued that by giving a privilege, the right to attend private school, only to those who belong to organized religions, the Court had violated the Establishment Clause in this decision. But this is not what the Court decided in these two early cases.

CONSCIENTIOUS OBJECTORS

A similar issue was raised in 1918 when the selective service law, which granted an exemption from the draft to ministers and theology students, was challenged as unconstitutional (*Selective Draft Law Cases*). The Court found the selective service law to be constitutional, because, at the time, the Court did not feel that this law violated the Establishment Clause.

During the 1960s and 1970s, the Supreme Court revisited this issue. In 1965, in *United States v. Seeger*, the question before the Court was one of statutory, not constitutional, interpretation. The Universal Military Training and Service Act exempted people who were conscientious objectors from military service if their objection was based on "religious training and belief." In this case three individuals were convicted of violating the law because they did not belong to a religious sect that believed war was wrong.

A unanimous Court ruled that anyone who held a "sincere and meaningful" religious belief against war would qualify for an exemption from the draft, even if he or she did not belong to a particular religious sect that preached pacifism. In this case the Court found the three men to be sincerely convinced that their personal religion forbade them to fight in a war. The justices thought that this sincere belief was all the statute required.

In 1970 the Court had to face up to the constitutional question in *Welsh v. United States*. The case involved a young man who had been sentenced to three years in prison for refusing to join the military when called by the draft board. This individual objected to war and fighting, but his objection was based on his personal philosophy, not on a religious belief. The issue before the justices was whether or not Congress could exempt from the draft people who objected to military service on the basis of their "religious" belief and not exempt people whose objection was based on beliefs that could not be called religious.

The issue was primarily whether this exemption violated the Establishment Clause by encouraging people to join religious sects in order to enjoy the privilege of not serving in the military. The practice also seemed to interfere with the freedom to hold beliefs, religious and otherwise, outside of the accepted religious groups. In this case, Elliot Welsh did not base his objection to war on his belief in a supreme being, but on his belief that all war was wrong.

Four justices thought that Welsh's belief was protected by the statute as written and that therefore the constitutional issue did not have to be discussed. Three justices thought that Welsh's belief did not satisfy the requirements of the statute, and that the statute was constitutional even if Welsh was not covered by it. Justice Blackmun did not participate in the decision. Justice Harlan was the swing vote, and he voted to free Mr. Welsh. Justice Harlan believed that the First Amendment prohibited Congress from exempting people from military service because of their religious beliefs without also exempting others whose belief was just as strong but was not based on religion. Congress could grant a "conscientious objection" exemption or take it away, but it could not condition the granting of the exemption on the holding of particular religious beliefs or on membership in particular religious groups.

In these conscientious objector cases, the Court ruled that laws could not grant privileges to members of organized religion that it did not grant to others in the society. If government granted a privilege based on religious belief, then it had to grant the same privilege to others who had similar beliefs, even if they did not belong to an organized religious group, and even if their beliefs were not based on anything that could be called religion. To rule otherwise would violate both the Establishment Clause, because it would encourage people to join religions in order to receive the privilege, and the Free Exercise Clause, because it would prevent people with a wide variety of religious and philosophical beliefs from being able to exercise those beliefs without interference.

EXEMPTION FROM COMPULSORY EDUCATION LAWS

That leads to the Supreme Court decision in the 1972 case of *Wisconsin v. Yoder* (see p. 105). This decision, with only Justice Douglas dissenting, was in many ways unique. The Amish people living in Wisconsin did not want to send their children to high school. They believed that an eighth grade education was sufficient for their needs and any further education would only corrupt their children. The Amish believe as part of their religion that people should lead a simple life on the farm.

This case was very different from the *Meyer* and *Society of Sisters* cases half a century before. The Amish were not asking for the right to send their children to a private Amish high school; they were asking that their children be exempted from the compulsory education laws altogether once they completed the eighth grade.

A Break from Precedent

Chief Justice Burger wrote the opinion for the Court. He ruled that the right to freely exercise religion included the right to keep children out of high school altogether. In coming to this conclusion, the chief justice seemed to abandon several central principles the Court had developed in interpreting the First Amendment.

Chief Justice Burger said that this right to keep children out of high school would not be granted to everyone who sincerely believed that high school was a bad thing; it would only be granted to people who held very strong "religious" beliefs that caused them to wish to stay away from high school. These people would have to belong to organized religious sects that could clearly justify this belief with their religion and show that the belief was central to their religion. This decision contradicted the decisions handed down in the conscientious objector cases, which held that to condition a privilege on the holding of a "religious" belief or membership in an organized religious sect violated the Establishment Clause.

Chief Justice Burger also seemed to abandon the distinction between belief and action that earlier decisions had turned on. In Chapter 5, we saw that the Court was willing to use the Free Exercise Clause to protect the right of the religious to believe whatever they want and to speak about those beliefs to others, even if others do not want to hear about those beliefs. At the same time, for many decades, the Court had refused to exempt the religious from general laws that prevented them from acting in ways that they believed their religion required them to act. The classic examples were cases decided in the second half of the 1800s, in which the Court ruled that Mormons did not have a right to practice polygamy if that practice violated the general criminal law. In Yoder, the Court allowed Amish parents to be exempt from the criminal laws that required parents to send their children to school until the children reached the age of 16.

Courts had uniformly held that religious beliefs did not exempt parents from the laws that required them to seek medical care for sick children, even if such medical care violated the religious beliefs of the parents. In the Yoder case, the Court allowed parents to withhold something equally important, education, because it interfered with the religious beliefs of the parents.

Justice Douglas was the only dissenter, and he did not object to the general conclusion of the decision. The right to attend or not attend public school, he believed, belonged to the students, not to the parents, and he emphasized that if any Amish children wished to attend high school, they should be allowed to do so. It was the children's right to religious freedom that counted in his opinion, not that of their parents.

The Establishment Clause and *Yoder*

A very good argument can be made against the Yoder decision. While the Court upheld the "religious freedom" rights of the Amish to practice their rural way of life, it did so in a way that violated the Establishment Clause. It granted a special privilege only to certain very special religious groups.

We have to imagine what was going through the mind of Chief Justice Burger as he wrote this opinion. The Amish had come to the United States long ago to avoid religious persecution in Europe. He could picture in his mind's eye the headlines around the world if the Amish moved out of the United States for the same reason after the U.S. Supreme Court had refused to acknowledge and protect their unique way of life. The Amish way of life does no harm to anyone, is in harmony with the environment, and could be considered a model of good citizenship by many people. We can certainly sympathize with his dilemma.

However, instead of basing his decision on the fact that the Amish are a very old and established religious group and therefore entitled to the privilege of keeping their children out of high school, Chief Justice Burger could have done what the Court did in *Society of Sisters*. He could have said that people who dedicate themselves to living a unique way of life outside of the mainstream, a way of life that involves living close to the land and without modern conveniences, can be exempt from laws that require them to send their children to high school. Of course this would mean allowing the children of the members of hippie communes to enjoy the same privilege, but that is the point. As the decision is written, the only way to enjoy this privilege is to join the Amish, which is clearly an encouragement to join a particular religion and therefore violates the Establishment Clause.

Chief Justice Burger also could have ruled that the Amish could create their own high school to provide education for their children until they reach the age of 16. This high school could concentrate on teaching the children things that would be helpful for their way of life. At the same time, the school would have to meet the reasonable educational standards of the state of Wisconsin. That is what we expect other religions to do if they object to having their children attend public high school. Why should the Amish be any different?

Do Children Have Rights?

There is another problem with the *Yoder* decision. Throughout the twentieth century, courts have ruled that there is a limit to the power parents can exercise over their children. American law has come to the conclusion that children have rights of their own. In the Pledge of Allegiance cases, for example, the Supreme Court affirmed the right of children to refuse to salute the flag. In other cases, courts have ruled that parents may not refuse to provide their children with modern medical aid, even if the parents do not believe in modern medicine. In *Yoder*, the Court seemed to say that the Amish may create a set of conditions, including limiting their children's education, that forces the

Amish children to remain in the sect when they reach adulthood. Doesn't this limit the right these children otherwise would have to make their own decisions about their religion and way of life once they reach adulthood? At the end of the twentieth century, it is difficult to imagine that someone would be able to get along very well with only an eighth grade education.

In fairness, there was no evidence in *Yoder* that any of the children involved wanted to attend high school. That raises an interesting question. What if some of the Amish children *did* want to attend high school? Would they have to sue their parents in order to have that right? What would the Court decide? Parents have a right to control their minor children, but children have a constitutional right to obtain an education, a right that goes back to the cases decided in the 1920s. Children today are suing their parents for parental malpractice. What if Amish children grew to adulthood and decided to move to a major American city and live in the modern world? They would find life in the modern world very difficult without a high school education. If the Amish children then sued their parents, could the parents defend themselves by saying that even the U.S. Supreme Court in *Yoder* had acknowledged their right to limit their children's education?

At the same time, defenders of the *Yoder* decision can argue that it does not really amount to much of a violation of the Establishment Clause because very few people actually join sects like the Amish in the twentieth century. Most members are born into the sects, and therefore the argument that this decision might encourage people to join these kinds of sects is not very convincing. Supporters of this decision might also say that accommodations could be made to Amish children who decided when they reached adulthood that they did want a high school education. Most communities have adult education programs and other programs designed to help all kinds of people who for one reason or another never finished high school. Many communities have special programs for new immigrants to American society, and people leaving the Amish society might be looked upon as new immigrants. They might have some difficulty, but with hard work they could integrate into mainstream society.

Education and Free Speech

The *Yoder* case also raises another issue that is ignored by the Court and the chief justice. One of the functions of high school education is to provide children with the tools to begin to think for themselves. In American society, we value the right of free speech and include within that right the right to hear and to learn because we believe that citizens should think for themselves. Our democratic political system depends on citizens being able to make their own decisions. Doesn't denying a high school education to these Amish children deprive them of these tools for making important decisions about their lives?

Supporters of the *Yoder* decision might respond that while this is a function of a public high school, many private religious high schools do not try to accomplish this goal, and the Amish high school could probably meet the requirements of the state of Wisconsin without providing tools for independent thinking. This leads back to the people of Oregon in the 1920s. They wanted all children to attend public school in order to make sure they did have these kinds of thinking tools. While we can object to the kind of "must go to public school" requirement that the Court ruled unconstitutional in *Pierce v. Society of Sisters* out of fear that public school might become simply a center to "brainwash" children into thinking a certain way, the same objection can be made of private religious schools. If the state does not have the right to "brainwash" children, should their parents have that right? In the 1920s few people questioned the right of parents to control the upbringing of their children. In the 1990s it is reasonable to say parents do not have the same kind of total control over the lives of their children that they enjoyed a century ago.

CONCLUSION

The Supreme Court ruled in the 1920s that every American has a right to obtain a private education, regardless of his or her religious beliefs. In 1970 the Court ruled that the government could not exempt people from compulsory military service because of their religious beliefs without providing a similar exemption to people who object to military service for personal nonreligious reasons.

In 1972, in *Wisconsin v. Yoder*, the Court ruled that some religious sects could receive an exemption from compulsory education laws, but only because of their unique religious beliefs. This decision appears to contradict other decisions which ruled that special exemptions for the religious violate the Establishment Clause. In the years since the *Yoder* decision was handed down, the Court has not extended the decision to any other situation. It appears that the Amish occupy a special position in both American society and constitutional history.

CASE DECISIONS

Pierce v. Society of Sisters and *Wisconsin v. Yoder* are concerned with whether or not parents have a right to control the education of their children. In the 1925 case of *Pierce v. Society of Sisters*, the Court ruled that parents have a constitutional right to send their children to private school, even religious private school. Justice McReynolds wrote the opinion for a unanimous court.

In 1972 Chief Justice Burger wrote the opinion in *Wisconsin v. Yoder*, which stands for the proposition that in some limited circumstances religious parents may keep their children out of school completely. Justices Stewart and White wrote short concurring opinions, which are not included here. Justice Douglas wrote a dissenting opinion, which is included here.

Following are excerpts from the case decisions.

* * * * * * * * * *

PIERCE v. SOCIETY OF SISTERS
268 U.S. 510 (1925)

MR. JUSTICE MCREYNOLDS delivered the opinion of the Court.

These appeals are from decrees, based upon undenied allegations, which granted preliminary orders restraining appellants from threatening or attempting to enforce the Compulsory Education Act adopted November 7, 1922, under the initiative provision of her Constitution by the voters of Oregon. . . .

The challenged Act, effective September 1, 1926, requires every parent, guardian or other person having control or charge or custody of a child between eight and sixteen years to send him "to a public school for the period of time a public school shall be held during the current year" in the district where the child resides; and failure so to do is declared a misdemeanor. . . .

Appellee, the Society of Sisters, is an Oregon corporation, organized in 1880, with power to care for orphans, educate and instruct the youth, establish and maintain academies or schools, and acquire necessary real and personal property. It has long devoted its property and effort to the secular and religious education and care of children, and has acquired the valuable good will of many parents and guardians. It conducts interdependent primary and high schools and junior colleges, and maintains orphanages for the custody and control of children between eight and sixteen. In its primary schools many children between those ages are taught the subjects usually pursued in Oregon public schools during the first eight years. Systematic religious instruction and moral training according to the tenets of the Roman Catholic Church are also regularly provided. . . .

After setting out the above facts the Society's bill alleges that the enactment conflicts with the right of parents to choose schools where their children will receive appropriate mental and religious training, the right of the child to influence the parents' choice of a school, the right of schools and teachers therein to engage in a useful business or profession, and is accordingly repugnant to the Constitution and void. And, further, that unless enforcement of the measure is enjoined the corporation's business and property will suffer irreparable injury. . . .

No question is raised concerning the power of the State reasonably to regulate all schools, to inspect, supervise and examine them, their teachers and pupils; to require that all children of proper age attend some school, that teachers shall be of good moral character and patriotic disposition, that certain studies plainly essential to good citizenship must be taught, and that nothing be taught which is manifestly inimical to the public welfare.

The inevitable practical result of enforcing the Act under consideration would be destruction of appellees' primary schools, and perhaps all other private primary schools for normal children within the State of Oregon. These parties are engaged in a kind of undertaking not inherently harmful, but long regarded as useful and meritorious. Certainly there is nothing in the present records to indicate that they have failed to discharge their obligations to patrons, students or the State. And there are no peculiar circumstances or present emergencies which demand extraordinary measures relative to primary education.

Under the doctrine of *Meyer v. Nebraska*, 262 U.S. 390, we think it entirely plain that the Act of 1922 unreasonably interferes with the liberty of parents and guardians to direct the upbringing and education of children under their control. As often heretofore pointed out, rights guaranteed by the Constitution may not be abridged by legislation which has no reasonable relation to some purpose within the competency of the State. The fundamental theory of liberty upon which all governments in this Union repose excludes any general power of the State to standardize its children by forcing them to accept instruction from public teachers only. The child is not the mere creature of the State; those who nurture him and direct his destiny have the right, coupled with the high duty, to recognize and prepare him for additional obligations. . . .

The suits were not premature. The injury to appellees was present and very real, not a mere possibility in the remote future. If no relief had been possible prior to the effective date of the Act, the injury would have become irreparable. Prevention of impending injury by unlawful action is a well recognized function of courts of equity.

The decrees below are

Affirmed.

WISCONSIN v. YODER
406 U.S. 205 (1972)

MR. CHIEF JUSTICE BURGER delivered the opinion of the Court.

On petition of the State of Wisconsin, we granted the writ of certiorari in this case to review a decision of the Wisconsin Supreme Court holding that respondents' convictions of violating the State's compulsory school-attendance law were invalid under the Free Exercise Clause of the First Amendment to the United States Constitution made applicable to the States by the Fourteenth Amendment. For the reasons hereafter stated we affirm the judgment of the Supreme Court of Wisconsin.

Respondents Jonas Yoder and Wallace Miller are members of the Old Order Amish religion, and respondent Adin Yutzy is a member of the Conservative Amish Mennonite Church. They and their families are residents of Green County, Wisconsin. Wisconsin's compulsory school-attendance law required them to cause their children to attend public or private school until reaching age 16 but the respondents declined to send their children, ages 14 and 15, to public school after they completed the eighth grade. The children were not enrolled in any private school, or within any recognized exception to the compulsory-attendance law, and they are conceded to be subject to the Wisconsin statute.

On complaint of the school district administrator for the public schools, respondents were charged, tried, and convicted of violating the compulsory-attendance law in Green County Court and were fined the sum of $5 each. Respondents defended on the ground that the application of the compulsory-attendance law violated their rights under the First and Fourteenth Amendments. The trial testimony showed that respondents believed, in accordance with the tenets of Old Order Amish communities generally, that their children's attendance at high school, public or private, was contrary to the Amish religion and way of life. They believed that by sending their children to high school, they would not only expose themselves to the danger of the censure of the church community, but, as found by the county court, also endanger their own salvation and that of their children. The State stipulated that respondents' religious beliefs were sincere.

In support of their position, respondents presented as expert witnesses scholars on religion and education whose testimony is uncontradicted. They expressed their opinions on the relationship of the Amish belief concerning school attendance to the more general tenets of their religion, and described the impact that compulsory high school attendance could have on the continued survival of Amish communities as they exist in the United States today. The history of the Amish sect was given in some detail, beginning with the Swiss Anabaptists of the 16th century who rejected institutionalized churches and sought to return to the early, simple, Christian life de-emphasizing material success, rejecting the competitive spirit, and seeking to insulate themselves from the modern world. As a result of their common heritage, Old Order Amish communities today are characterized by a fundamental belief that salvation requires life in a church community separate and apart from the world and worldly influence. This concept of life aloof from the world and its values is central to their faith. . . .

Amish objection to formal education beyond the eighth grade is firmly grounded in these central religious concepts. They object to the high school, and higher education generally, because the values they teach are in marked variance with Amish values and the Amish way of life; they view secondary school education as an impermissible exposure of their children to a "worldly" influence in conflict with their beliefs. The high school tends to emphasize intellectual and scientific accomplishments, self-distinction, competitiveness, worldly success, and social life with other students. Amish society emphasizes informal learning-through-doing; a life of "goodness," rather than a life of intellect; wisdom, rather than technical knowledge; community welfare, rather than competition; and separation from, rather than integration with, contemporary worldly society. . . .

We come then to the quality of the claims of the respondents concerning the alleged encroachment of Wisconsin's compulsory school-attendance statute on their rights and the rights of their children to the free exercise of the religious beliefs they and their forebears have adhered to for almost three centuries. In evaluating those claims we must be careful to determine whether the Amish religious faith and their mode of life are, as they claim, inseparable and interdependent. A way of life, however virtuous and admirable, may not be interposed as a barrier to reasonable state regulation of education if it is based on purely secular considerations; to have the protection of the Religion Clauses, the claims must be rooted in religious belief. Although a determination of what is a "religious" belief or practice entitled to constitutional protection may present a most delicate question, the very concept of ordered liberty precludes allowing every person to make his own standards on matters of conduct in which society as a whole has important interests. Thus, if the Amish asserted their claims because of their subjective evaluation and rejection of the contemporary secular values accepted by the majority, much as Thoreau rejected the social values of his time and isolated himself at Walden Pond, their claims would not rest on a religious basis. Thoreau's choice was philosophical and personal rather than religious, and such belief does not rise to the demands of the Religion Clauses.

Giving no weight to such secular considerations, however, we see that the record in this case abundantly supports the claim that the traditional way of life of the Amish is not merely a matter of personal preference, but one of deep religious conviction, shared by an organized group, and intimately related to daily living. That the Old Order Amish daily life and religious practice stem from their faith is shown by the fact that it is in response to their literal interpretation of the Biblical injunction from the Epistle of Paul to the Romans, "be not conformed to this world. . . ." This command is fundamental to the Amish faith. Moreover, for the Old Order Amish, religion is not simply a matter of theocratic belief. As the expert witnesses explained, the Old Order Amish religion pervades and determines virtually their entire way of life, regulating it with the detail of the Talmudic diet through the strictly enforced rules of the church community. . . .

Neither the findings of the trial court nor the Amish claims as to the nature of their faith are challenged in this Court by the State of Wisconsin. Its position is that the State's interest in universal compulsory formal secondary education to age 16 is so great that it is paramount to the undisputed claims of respondents that their mode of preparing their youth for Amish life, after the traditional elementary education, is an essential part of their religious belief and practice. Nor does the State undertake to meet the claim that the Amish mode of life and education is inseparable from and a part of the basic tenets of their religion—indeed, as much a part of their religious belief and practices as baptism, the confessional, or a sabbath may be for others.

Wisconsin concedes that under the Religion Clauses religious beliefs are absolutely free from the State's control, but it argues that "actions," even though religiously grounded, are outside the protection of the First Amendment. But our decisions have rejected the idea that religiously grounded conduct is always outside the protection of the Free Exercise Clause. It is true that activities of individuals, even when religiously based, are often subject to regulation by the States in the exercise of their undoubted power to promote the health, safety, and general welfare, or the Federal Government in the exercise of its delegated powers. . . .

The State attacks respondents' position as one fostering "ignorance" from which the child must be protected by the State. No one can question the State's duty to protect children from ignorance but this argument does not square with the facts disclosed in the record. Whatever their idiosyncrasies as seen by the majority, this record strongly shows that the Amish community has been a highly successful social unit within our society, even if apart from the conventional "mainstream." Its members are productive and very law-abiding members of society; they reject public welfare in any of its usual modern forms. The Congress itself recognized their self-sufficiency by authorizing exemption of such groups as the Amish from the obligation to pay social security taxes. . . .

For the reasons stated we hold, with the Supreme Court of Wisconsin, that the First and Fourteenth Amendments prevent the State from compelling respondents to cause their children to attend formal high school to age 16. Our disposition of this case, however, in no way alters our recognition of the obvious fact that courts are not school boards or legislatures, and are ill-equipped to determine the "necessity" of discrete aspects of a State's program of compulsory education. This should suggest that courts must move with great circumspection in performing the sensitive and delicate task of weighing a

State's legitimate social concern when faced with religious claims for exemption from generally applicable educational requirements. It cannot be overemphasized that we are not dealing with a way of life and mode of education by a group claiming to have recently discovered some "progressive" or more enlightened process for rearing children for modern life.

Aided by a history of three centuries as an identifiable religious sect and a long history as a successful and self-sufficient segment of American society, the Amish in this case have convincingly demonstrated the sincerity of their religious beliefs, the interrelationship of belief with their mode of life, the vital role that belief and daily conduct play in the continued survival of Old Order Amish communities and their religious organization, and the hazards presented by the State's enforcement of a statute generally valid as to others. Beyond this, they have carried the even more difficult burden of demonstrating the adequacy of their alternative mode of continuing informal vocational education in terms of precisely those overall interests that the State advances in support of its program of compulsory high school education. In light of this convincing showing, one that probably few other religious groups or sects could make, and weighing the minimal difference between what the State would require and what the Amish already accept, it was incumbent on the State to show with more particularity how its admittedly strong interest in compulsory education would be adversely affected by granting an exception to the Amish. *Sherbert v. Verner, supra.*

Nothing we hold is intended to undermine the general applicability of the State's compulsory school-attendance statutes or to limit the power of the State to promulgate reasonable standards that, while not impairing the free exercise of religion, provide for continuing agricultural vocational education under parental and church guidance by the Old Order Amish or others similarly situated. The States have had a long history of amicable and effective relationships with church-sponsored schools, and there is no basis for assuming that, in this related context, reasonable standards cannot be established concerning the content of the continuing vocational education of Amish children under parental guidance, provided always that state regulations are not inconsistent with what we have said in this opinion.

Affirmed.

Dissenting Opinion   MR. JUSTICE DOUGLAS, dissenting in part.

I agree with the Court that the religious scruples of the Amish are opposed to the education of their children beyond the grade schools, yet I disagree with the Court's conclusion that the matter is within the dispensation of parents alone. The Court's analysis assumes that the only interests at stake in the case are those of the Amish parents on the one hand, and those of the State on the other. The difficulty with this approach is that, despite the Court's claim, the parents are seeking to vindicate not only their own free exercise claims, but also those of their high-school-age children. . . .

It is the future of the student, not the future of the parents, that is imperiled by today's decision. If a parent keeps his child out of school beyond the grade school, then the child will be forever barred from entry into the new and amazing world of diversity that we have today. The child may decide that that is the preferred course, or he may rebel. It is the student's judgment, not his parents', that is essential if we are to give full meaning to what we have said about the Bill of Rights and of the right of students to be masters of their own destiny. If he is harnessed to the Amish way of life by those in authority over him and if his education is truncated, his entire life may be stunted and deformed. The child, therefore, should be given an opportunity to be heard before the State gives the exemption which we honor today.

The views of the two children in question were not canvassed by the Wisconsin courts. The matter should be explicitly reserved so that new hearings can be held on remand of the case.

I think the emphasis of the Court on the "law and order" record of this Amish group of people is quite irrelevant. A religion is a religion irrespective of what the misdemeanor or felony records of its members might be. I am not at all sure how the Catholics, Episcopalians, the Baptists, Jehovah's Witnesses, the Unitarians, and my own Presbyterians would make out if subjected to such a test. It is, of course, true that if a group or society was organized to perpetuate crime and if that is its motive, we would have rather startling problems akin to those that were raised when some years back a particular sect was challenged here as operating on a fraudulent basis. *United States v. Ballard*, 322 U.S. 78. But no such factors are present here, and the Amish, whether with a high or low criminal record, certainly qualify by all historic standards as a religion within the meaning of the First Amendment.

The Court rightly rejects the notion that actions, even though religiously grounded, are always outside the protection of the Free Exercise Clause of the First Amendment. In so ruling, the Court departs from the teaching of *Reynolds v. United States*, 98 U.S. 145, 164, where it was said concerning the reach of the Free Exercise Clause of the First Amendment, "Congress was deprived of all legislative power over mere opinion, but was left free to reach actions which were in violation of social duties or subversive of good order." In that case it was conceded that polygamy was a part of the religion of the Mormons. Yet the Court said, "It matters not that his belief [in polygamy] was a part of his professed religion: it was still belief, and belief only." *Id.*, at 167.

Action, which the Court deemed to be antisocial, could be punished even though it was grounded on deeply held and sincere religious convictions. What we do today, at least in this respect, opens the way to give organized religion a broader base than it has ever enjoyed; and it even promises that in time *Reynolds* will be overruled.

.............................DISCUSSION QUESTIONS ....

1. The right to seek out knowledge is not specifically mentioned in the Bill of Rights. At the same time, it could be said that this right is implied by the right of free speech. How would you make such an argument? Do you think it is right to "imply" some rights from others specifically mentioned in the Bill of Rights?
2. In *Meyer v. Nebraska*, Nebraska argued that children should learn English before learning other languages. The majority of justices believed that learning other languages at an early age did not do any harm, and that only if languages were taught early could they ever really be mastered. If we had a lot of scientific evidence that Nebraska was right and that learning more than one language before the age of 14 really was harmful, do you think the decision would have been any different?
3. In your opinion, are there any subjects that the government could make illegal to teach in a private school?
4. Do you think that the government could stop a group of Satan worshipers from sending their children to a private school that taught Satan worship?
5. What arguments can you make in support of and against the U.S. Supreme Court decision in the *Wisconsin v. Yoder* case? In what ways is the *Yoder* decision unique?

CHAPTER
seven
• • • • • • • • •

When Religion Conflicts
with the Law

.... DISCUSSION ....

The First Amendment protects the right to freely exercise religion, but what exactly does the right to freely exercise religion mean? As we have seen in the previous chapters, this right means that religious people have the right to *believe* whatever they want to believe without interference from government, even interference in the form of a forced Pledge of Allegiance to the flag. The right to freely exercise religion also means that religious people have the right to *speak* to others about their religious beliefs without unreasonable government interference, even if their speech is a nuisance to others. The difficult question has been: Does the right to freely exercise religion include the right to *do* something that is otherwise a violation of the criminal law?

POLYGAMY

The first Supreme Court decision to deal with this issue came in 1878. The case, *Reynolds v. United States* (see p. 120), involved the question of whether Mormons could have more than one wife, in violation of federal law. Federal law applied to Utah at the time because Utah was a territory. (Utah did not become a state until 1896.) A Mormon man, convicted of violating the laws against polygamy, appealed his conviction to the U.S. Supreme Court. He argued that his conviction had to be overturned because the law against polygamy interfered with his right to freely practice his religion.

The members of the Supreme Court were called upon to interpret this section of the First Amendment for the first time. They examined the writings of Thomas Jefferson on the subject and concluded that the right to freely exercise religion included the "right of conscience" and the right to hold and speak about "heretical opinions," but it did not include the right to "do" things that would otherwise violate the criminal law.

Chief Justice Waite wrote the opinion for a unanimous Court. In looking at the history of the First Amendment, he was particularly impressed by the influence James Madison and Thomas Jefferson had had on the writing of the amendment. The main purpose of the religion clauses of the First Amendment, Chief Justice Waite decided, was to achieve the same result as the Bill for Establishing Religious Freedom in Virginia had a few years before. That law clearly protected the right to believe and to profess a belief, but it did not protect the right to engage in "overt acts" that might violate the criminal law.

Polygamy had always been "odious" to the nations of Europe, Chief Justice Waite noted, and polygamy had been a capital offense in England since the time of James I. Because polygamy had been a crime in the United States both before and after the passage of the First Amendment, clearly none of the people who voted to pass the First Amendment into law thought that the amendment prevented the enforcement of laws such as this.

The members of the Court then raised two points that have continued to be important in any discussion of whether religious people acting on their religious beliefs can violate criminal law. First, if people were allowed to violate the criminal law without punishment because they acted in the name of religion, then there would be one law for the religious and another law for everyone else. In a very real sense, the religious would have a privilege not enjoyed by other people. Would this not be a violation of the Establishment Clause in that people who wished to violate a particular law would be encouraged to join a religion that advocated that particular behavior?

Second, if the Court were to accept this idea of one law for the religious and another for everyone else, where would it draw the line? What crimes would the religious be allowed to commit in the name of religion? In order to put the issue into sharper focus, the justices asked the ultimate question: "Suppose one believed that human sacrifice were a necessary part of religious worship, would it seriously be contended that the civil government under which we live could not interfere to prevent a sacrifice?" Attorneys and judges often use this technique (asking what they consider to be the ultimate question) to clarify issues. If the answer to this question was no (and it was clear to all the members of the Court in 1878 that the only answer to this question was no), then where would the Court draw the line? The Supreme Court did not want to have to hear hundreds of cases, deciding which behaviors were minor and could be exempted from the criminal law on religious grounds, and which behaviors were too terrible and could not be so exempted.

Chief Justice Waite argued that to allow someone to defend against criminal prosecution in this way would introduce "a new element into criminal law." It would in a sense allow everyone to become a "law unto himself," and government would exist in name only. Chief Justice Waite could see only chaos ahead if the Court allowed the Mormons to avoid the law against polygamy on the ground that their religion required them to practice polygamy.

In 1890 the Court again ruled that Mormons could not engage in polygamy and avoid prosecution under the criminal law (*Davis v. Beason*). In their decision, the justices felt it necessary to note that polygamy "degrades women" and "debases men," and that "few crimes are more pernicious to the best interests of society." Again, the justices felt that the right to freely exercise religion protected "belief" but not "behavior."

MIRACULOUS CLAIMS AND FRAUD

As discussed in Chapter 5, from 1940 to 1953 the Court heard a series of cases involving Jehovah's Witnesses and the need religions have to solicit funds and to distribute or sell literature in order to spread their beliefs. Both the right of free speech and the right to freely exercise religion were involved in these cases, and the Court felt that some laws had to be declared unconstitutional in order to protect these rights. Although not discussed in these decisions, we presume that other citizens would have the same rights that the Court granted in these cases to the Jehovah's Witnesses if they wanted to discuss things other than religion. Presumably a political group would be allowed to solicit funds, pass out literature, ring doorbells, and make a public address in a city park. While the right to freely exercise religion was involved in these cases, this was not an area where one law would apply to the religious and another to everyone else. Everyone else would also have the right to make a nuisance of themselves in order to have their ideas heard by their fellow citizens.

All of these cases involved the right to speak, and the Court felt that the general right of free speech, and the specific right to freely exercise religion, required that government could not interfere in these situations. In 1944 the Court was faced with a very difficult case, *United States v. Ballard*, and split five to four. The case involved the conviction of the Ballard family for mail fraud. The Ballards had created the "I Am" religious movement. As part of their effort to find converts, they sent material through the mail that suggested that Guy Ballard had talked with Saint Germain and that the saint had selected Mr. Ballard to be his divine messenger here on earth. The material also stated that the Ballards had been able to heal people through faith alone and that they had other miraculous powers.

The Ballards were charged with the crime of fraud. Fraud is committed when someone tells a lie, knowing at the time that it is a lie, in order to get money.

At the trial the judge told the members of the jury that their job was not to determine whether what the Ballards said happened actually had happened, but rather to determine whether or not the Ballards actually believed "in good faith" that what they said happened actually had happened.

Justice Douglas, writing for the five-justice majority, threw out the convictions. He ruled that the free exercise clause prevented the criminal prosecution of anyone for fraud based on discussions of religion. He said:

> [T]he miracles of the New Testament, the Divinity of Christ, life after death, the power of prayers are deep in the religious convictions of many. If one could be sent to jail because a jury in a hostile environment found those teachings false, little indeed would be left of religious freedom.

One purpose of the Free Exercise Clause, Justice Douglas believed, was to give the "widest possible toleration of conflicting views" on the subject of religion. While the Ballards' statements and beliefs may seem "preposterous" to most people, if their beliefs could be put on trial before a jury charged with finding "their truth or falsity," then the same could be done to the statements and beliefs of any religious group.

Chief Justice Stone, one of the four dissenters, stated that he was

> not prepared to say that the constitutional guaranty of freedom of religion affords immunity from criminal prosecution for the fraudulent procurement of money by false statements as to one's religious experiences, more than it renders polygamy or libel immune from criminal prosecution.

Chief Justice Stone was outvoted in this case. The Ballards would go free because they had a right under the Constitution to say anything they wanted to say as long as they were discussing matters of religion. Just as the Jehovah's Witnesses could solicit funds and pass out literature, so the members of the "I Am" movement were free to mail out literature saying they had spoken with a saint and healed people with prayer, regardless of whether or not any of these things actually had happened and regardless of whether or not the Ballards actually believed that these things had happened.

In discussing this case, we must keep in mind that to make a case of fraud, the prosecution must prove not only that someone told untruths in order to get money or property, but also that he or she knew that what he or she was saying was untrue. Because of this, the Ballard case involved not only the question of speech but also the issue of belief. Can government be allowed to pry into people's beliefs with the force of the criminal law?

Justice Jackson wrote his own opinion agreeing that the convictions should be overturned. If some members of the "I Am" movement received comfort from the thought that they were being watched over by Saint Germain, he asked, then who is to say that they did not get exactly what they paid for? He went on to say:

> The wrong of these things, as I see it, is not in the money the victims part with half as much as in the mental and spiritual poison they get. But that is precisely the thing the Constitution put beyond the reach of the prosecutor, for the price of freedom of religion or of speech or of the press is that we must put up with, and even pay for, a good deal of rubbish. Prosecutions of this character easily could degenerate into religious persecution. I do not doubt that religious leaders may be convicted of fraud for making false representations on matters other than faith or experience, as for example if one represents that funds are being used to construct a church when in fact they are being used for personal purposes. But that is not this case . . .

The distinction Justice Jackson drew between making statements concerning "faith or experience" versus making statements concerning how money would be spent still holds. The Reverend Jim Bakker went to prison in the 1980s because he sold more rooms in his hotel than he actually built, not because he promised people a passport to heaven.

SCHOOL ATTENDANCE LAWS

In 1972 the Burger Court also exempted some people from criminal prosecution for violating the criminal law because of their religious beliefs. The case was *Wisconsin v. Yoder* (see p. 105), discussed in Chapter 6. The Amish parents in this case wished to stop their children's education after the eighth grade in violation of Wisconsin criminal law, which required that children attend school until the age of 16 (and which put parents in jail if their children did not attend). The Supreme Court agreed that the Amish could keep their children out of school, but only because the children belonged to a very special religious group that required them to live a very simple life. In the opinion of the Court and the Amish parents, the Amish way of life made further education irrelevant, and possibly harmful, to these children.

In handing down the decision in *Yoder*, Chief Justice Burger had to abandon for a time the idea that people should not have to belong to organized religious groups in order to enjoy the benefits of the Free Exercise Clause. He said that only the members of very old and legitimate religious groups would be allowed to violate the compulsory education laws in this way. He also abandoned for a time the idea that the Free Exercise Clause protected the right to believe and speak but not the right to act on those beliefs. In this case the Amish parents had acted on their beliefs and were exempt from prosecution.

At the same time, it can be argued that there is a difference between committing the technical crime of keeping children out of school and committing a positive act of criminal behavior. Keeping children home to protect them from what their parents believe will be harmful education is different from performing a human sacrifice or committing polygamy. However, this decision raises the question Chief Justice Waite raised in the *Reynolds* case: Where does the Court draw the line? What other illegal things can the religious do because they honestly believe harm will result if they do not?

PEYOTE USE IN RELIGIOUS CEREMONIES

The 1990 case of *Employment Division v. Smith* (see p. 125), involved two drug rehabilitation counselors who were fired when they ingested peyote, a hallucinogenic drug, as part of a religious ceremony performed by the Native American Church. After they were fired, they applied for unemployment compensation from the state of Oregon but were turned down. Generally, people who are fired because they commit acts of misconduct are not entitled to unemployment compensation. The state agency in charge of unemployment compensation felt that it was misconduct for drug counselors to ingest illegal drugs.

The Oregon Supreme Court ruled that to deny these two their unemployment compensation violated their right to freely exercise their religion. The Oregon Supreme Court also ruled that to the extent that Oregon law made the ingestion of peyote a crime, that law was unconstitutional as applied to a situation such as this.

This put the issue of whether the Free Exercise Clause can be interpreted to exempt someone from the general criminal laws directly before the U.S. Supreme Court. The Court voted five to three that it could not (with a special opinion by Justice O'Connor). Just as over a century before, in *Reynolds v. United States*, Mr. Reynolds was not free to violate the polygamy laws, so these drug counselors were not free to violate the drug laws in the name of religion.

Justice Scalia wrote the opinion for the five-justice majority. He pointed out that in previous Supreme Court cases, when action had been exempted from the law it had involved protecting the right to "believe" or to "speak," not the right to "behave." The Jehovah's Witnesses cases had involved soliciting money and passing out literature, which were fundamentally different from ingesting peyote in violation of the drug laws.

The two drug counselors argued that the Court should balance their religious beliefs against the government's interest when enforcing a particular law. Justice Scalia rejected this argument, saying:

To make an individual's obligation to obey such a law contingent upon the law's coincidence with his religious beliefs, except where the State's interest is "compelling"—permitting him, by virtue of his beliefs, "to become a law unto himself," (citing *Reynolds*)—contradicts both constitutional tradition and common sense.

The drug counselors argued that government would only have to prove that a criminal law served a "compelling" interest if the behavior engaged in was "central" to the person's religious beliefs. Justice Scalia rejected this idea, because it would force judges to decide whether or not something was central to someone's religious beliefs. He asked: "What principle of law or logic can be brought to bear to contradict a believer's assertion that a particular act is 'central' to his personal faith?"

Three dissenting justices were ready to allow these drug counselors to be exempt from this particular criminal law. These justices thought that, before the state could convict a religious person of committing a crime when the behavior involved was required by beliefs central to the person's religion, the state should have to prove that the law that had been violated served a compelling state interest. This reasoning raised the troubling possibility that there would be a religious defense for every so-called victimless crime, from polygamy and drug abuse to prostitution and gambling. How compelling must the state's interest be and how central must the particular behavior be to the person's religious beliefs in order to justify an exemption from the criminal law? Wouldn't the Court be tempted to grant exemptions to older religious groups and not to new religious sects, and wouldn't this be a violation of the Establishment Clause?

Justice O'Connor wrote her own opinion, in which she agreed that the two drug counselors should not get unemployment compensation, but she did not agree with Justice Scalia's reasoning. She thought, along with the dissenters, that the Court should weigh the government's need for a law against the importance of the particular behavior in a person's religion. In this case she felt that the government's need to stop drug use was "compelling," and therefore in this case the government would win even if such a balancing test were used. (The three dissenting justices did not agree with her and felt the balance would go in favor of the drug users.)

This was a controversial decision, and many religious groups asked Congress to pass legislation to overturn it, but that was not easy to do. What would this legislation say? What kinds of behavior would be exempted from the working of the criminal law in the name of religion? Wouldn't such a law run afoul of the Establishment Clause in that it would appear to favor certain religious groups and the religious over the nonreligious? Congress passed such a law in November 1993, but it remains to be seen how it will be interpreted.

RELIGIOUS SACRIFICE OF ANIMALS

On June 11, 1993, a unanimous Court decided that laws that make behavior criminal only if performed for a religious purpose are generally going to violate the Free Exercise Clause of the First Amendment. The case, *Church of Lukumi Babalu Aye v. Hialeah,* involved members of the Santeria religion who wished to build a church in the city of Hialeah, Florida. In an attempt to stop this sect from building a church, the city passed an ordinance making the "ritual sacrifice" of animals a criminal offense. It was still legal to "slaughter" animals but not to "sacrifice" them. Justice Kennedy, writing the opinion for the court, pointed out that in *Employment Division v. Smith* the Court had held that people could not be exempted from "neutral, generally applicable" laws because of their religion. This law in Hialeah was the opposite of a "neutral, generally applicable" law. Rather than outlawing the killing of animals in general, the law made the killing of animals a crime only if it was performed for a "religious" purpose. The obvious purpose of the law was to prevent members of the Santeria religion from building a church in the city. The Court ruled that this law violated the Free Exercise Clause.

CONCLUSION

The problem that Chief Justice Waite raised in 1878 in *Reynolds* still exists. Where does the Court draw the line? Would the Supreme Court have to hear hundreds of cases in which the "compelling" interests of government were weighed against the "central" beliefs of various religious sects? Would the result of this balancing act change over time as new justices were added to the Court? In the case of *Employment Division v. Smith,* Justice O'Connor performed such a balancing test and found in favor of the state. Justices Blackmun, Brennan, and Marshall performed the same balancing test and found in favor of the religious sect. How would judges below the level of the Supreme Court ever be able to sort this out?

The answer is that they will not have to try. Five justices in the *Employment Division v. Smith* case decided that this would simply not be practical. While the Free Exercise Clause protects the right to believe and speak about religious beliefs, it does not protect the right to have two wives or to take illegal drugs. The distinction between belief and action was drawn in 1878 and is still the law in the 1990s.

......................................CASE DECISIONS ....

Reynolds v. United States and *Employment Division v. Smith* are concerned with the extent to which religious individuals may be excused from the workings of the criminal law when they are acting on their religious beliefs. The sections of the majority opinion in the case of *Reynolds v. United States* that are concerned with this issue are included here. A unanimous Supreme Court agreed in this 1878 case that religious belief did not excuse criminal behavior.

In 1990 the Court faced this issue again in the case of *Employment Division v. Smith*. Justice Scalia wrote the opinion for the majority of the justices who again ruled that religious belief does not excuse criminal conduct. Three justices dissented. Justice O'Connor wrote a concurring opinion and Justice Blackmun wrote a dissenting opinion, which are also included here.

Following are excerpts from the case decisions.

● ● ● ● ● ● ● ● ● ●

REYNOLDS v. UNITED STATES
98 U.S. 145 (1878)

MR. CHIEF JUSTICE WAITE delivered the opinion of the court. . . .

On the trial, the plaintiff in error, the accused, proved that at the time of his alleged second marriage he was, and for many years before had been, a member of the Church of Jesus Christ of Latter-Day Saints, commonly called the Mormon Church, and a believer in its doctrines; that it was an accepted doctrine of that church "that it was the duty of male members of said church, circumstances permitting, to practise polygamy; . . . that this duty was enjoined by different books which the members of said church believed to be of divine origin, and among others the Holy Bible, and also that the members of the church believed that the practice of polygamy was directly enjoined upon the male members thereof by the Almighty God, in a revelation to Joseph Smith, the founder and prophet of said church; that the failing or refusing to practise polygamy by such male members of said church, when circumstances would admit, would be punished, and that the penalty for such failure and refusal would be damnation in the life to come." He also proved "that he had received permission from the recognized authorities in said church to enter into polygamous marriage; . . . that Daniel H. Wells, one having authority in said church to perform the marriage ceremony, married the said defendant on or about the time the crime is alleged to have been committed, to some woman by the name of Schofield, and that such marriage ceremony was performed under and pursuant to the doctrines of said church."

Upon this proof he asked the court to instruct the jury that if they found from the evidence that he "was married as charged—if he was married—in pursuance of and in conformity with what he believed at the time to be a religious duty, that the verdict must be 'not guilty.'" This request was refused, and the court did charge "that there must have been a criminal intent, but that if the defendant, under the influence of a religious belief that it was right,—under an inspiration, if you please, that it was right,—deliberately married a second time, having a first wife living, the want of consciousness of evil intent—the want of understanding on his part that he was committing a crime—did not excuse him; but the law inexorably in such case implies the criminal intent."

Upon this charge and refusal to charge the question is raised, whether religious belief can be accepted as a justification of an overt act made criminal by the law of the land. The inquiry is not as to the power of Congress to prescribe criminal laws for the Territories, but as to the guilt of one who knowingly violates a law which has been properly enacted, if he entertains a religious belief that the law is wrong.

Congress cannot pass a law for the government of the Territories which shall prohibit the free exercise of religion. The first amendment to the Constitution expressly forbids such legislation. Religious freedom is guaranteed everywhere throughout the United States, so far as congressional interference is concerned. The question to be determined is, whether the law now under consideration comes within this prohibition.

The word "religion" is not defined in the Constitution. We must go elsewhere, therefore, to ascertain its meaning, and nowhere more appropriately, we think, than to the history of the times in the midst of which the provision was adopted. The precise point of the inquiry is, what is the religious freedom which has been guaranteed.

Before the adoption of the Constitution, attempts were made in some of the colonies and States to legislate not only in respect to the establishment of religion, but in respect to its doctrines and precepts as well. The people were taxed, against their will, for the support of religion, and sometimes for the support of particular sects to whose tenets they could not and did not subscribe. Punishments were prescribed for a failure to attend upon public worship, and sometimes for entertaining heretical opinions. The controversy upon this general subject was animated in many of the States, but seemed at last to culminate in Virginia. In 1784, the House of Delegates of that State having under consideration "a bill establishing provision for teachers of the Christian religion," postponed it until the next session, and directed that the bill should be published and distributed, and that the people be requested "to signify their opinion respecting the adoption of such a bill at the next session of assembly."

This brought out a determined opposition. Amongst others, Mr. Madison prepared a "Memorial and Remonstrance," which was widely circulated and signed, and in which he demonstrated "that religion, or the duty we owe the Creator," was not within the cognizance of civil government. Semple's Virginia Baptists, Appendix. At the next session the proposed bill was not only defeated, but another, "for establishing religious freedom," drafted by Mr. Jefferson, was passed. 1 Jeff. Works, 45; 2 Howison, Hist. of Va. 298. In the preamble of this act (12 Hening's Stat. 84) religious freedom is defined; and after a recital "that to suffer the civil magistrate to intrude his powers into the field of opinion, and to restrain the profession or propagation of principles on supposition of their ill tendency, is a dangerous fallacy which at once destroys all religious liberty," it is declared "that it is time enough for the rightful purposes of civil government for its officers to interfere when principles break out into overt acts against peace and good order." In these two sentences is found the true distinction between what properly belongs to the church and what to the State.

In a little more than a year after the passage of this statute the convention met which prepared the Constitution of the United States. Of this convention Mr. Jefferson was not a member, he being then absent as minister to France. As soon as he saw the draft of the Constitution proposed for adoption, he, in a letter to a friend, expressed his disappointment at the absence of an express declaration insuring the freedom of religion (2 Jeff. Works, 355), but was willing to accept it as it was, trusting that the good sense and honest intentions of the people would bring about the necessary alterations. 1 Jeff. Works, 79. Five of the States, while adopting the Constitution, proposed amendments. Three—New Hampshire, New York, and Virginia—included in one form or another a declaration of religious freedom in the changes they desired to have made, as did also North Carolina, where the convention at first declined to ratify the Constitution until the proposed amendments were acted upon. Accordingly, at the first session of the first Congress the amendment now under consideration was proposed with others by Mr. Madison. It met the views of the advocates of religious freedom, and was adopted. Mr. Jefferson afterwards, in reply to an address to him by a committee of the Danbury Baptist Association (8 id. 113), took occasion to say: "Believing with you that religion is a matter which lies solely between man and his God; that he owes account to none other for his faith or his worship; that the legislative powers of the government reach actions only, and not opinions,—I contemplate with sovereign reverence that act of the whole American people which declared that their legislature should 'make no law respecting an establishment of religion or prohibiting the free exercise thereof,' thus building a wall of separation between church and State. Adhering to this expression of the supreme will of the nation in behalf of the rights of conscience, I shall see with sincere satisfaction the progress of those sentiments which tend to restore man to all his natural rights, convinced he has no natural right in opposition to his social duties." Coming as this does from an acknowledged leader of the advocates of the measure, it may be accepted almost as an authoritative declaration of the scope and effect of the amendment thus secured. Congress was deprived of all legislative power over mere opinion, but was left free to reach actions which were in violation of social duties or subversive of good order.

Polygamy has always been odious among the northern and western nations of Europe, and, until the establishment of the Mormon Church, was almost exclusively a feature of the life of Asiatic and of African people. At common law, the second marriage was always void (2 Kent, Com. 79), and from the earliest history of England polygamy has been treated as an offense against society. After the establishment of the ecclesiastical courts, and until the time of James I., it was punished through the instrumentality of those tribunals, not merely because ecclesiastical rights had been violated, but because upon the separation of the ecclesiastical courts from the civil the ecclesiastical were supposed to be the most appropriate for the trial of matrimonial causes and offences against the rights of marriage, just as they were for testamentary causes and the settlement of the estates of deceased persons.

By the statute of 1 James I. (c. 11), the offence, if committed in England or Wales, was made punishable in the civil courts, and the penalty was death. As this statute was limited in its operation to England and Wales, it was at a very early period re-enacted, generally with some modifications, in all the colonies. In connection with the case we are now considering, it is a significant fact that on the 8th of December, 1788, after the passage of the act establishing religious freedom, and after the convention of Virginia had recommended as an amendment to the Constitution of the United States the declaration in a bill of rights that "all men have an equal, natural, and unalienable right to the free exercise of religion, according to the dictates of conscience," the legislature of that State substantially enacted the statute of James I., death penalty included, because, as recited in the preamble, "it hath been doubted whether bigamy or poligamy be punishable by the laws of this Commonwealth." 12 Hening's Stat. 691. From that day to this we think it may safely be said there never has been a time in any State of the Union when polygamy has not been an offence against society, cognizable by the civil courts and punishable with more or less severity. In the face of all this evidence, it is impossible to believe that the constitutional guaranty of religious freedom was intended to prohibit legislation in respect to this most important feature of social life. Marriage, while from its very nature a sacred obligation, is nevertheless, in most civilized nations, a civil contract, and usually regulated by law. Upon it society may be said to be built, and out of its fruits spring social relations and social obligations and duties, with which government is necessarily required to deal. In fact, according as monogamous or polygamous marriages are allowed, do we find the principles on which the government of the people, to a greater or less extent, rests. Professor Lieber says, polygamy leads to the patriarchial principle, and which, when applied to large communities, fetters the people in stationary despotism, while that principle cannot long exist in connection with monogamy. Chancellor Kent observes that this remark is equally striking and profound. 2 Kent, Com. 81, note (e). An exceptional colony of polygamists under an exceptional leadership may sometimes exist for a time without appearing to disturb the social condition of the people who surround it; but there cannot be a doubt that, unless restricted by some form of constitution, it is within the legitimate scope of the power of every civil government to determine whether polygamy or monogamy shall be the law of social life under its dominion.

In our opinion, the statute immediately under consideration is within the legislative power of Congress. It is constitutional and valid as prescribing a rule of action for all those residing in the Territories, and in places over which the United States have exclusive control. This being so, the only question which remains is, whether those who make polygamy a part of their religion are excepted from the operation of the statute. If they are, then those who do not make polygamy a part of their religious belief may be found guilty and punished, while those who do, must be acquitted and go free. This would be introducing a new element into criminal law. Laws are made for the government of actions, and while they cannot interfere with mere religious belief and opinions, they may with practices. Suppose one believed that human sacrifices were a necessary part of religious worship, would it be seriously contended that the civil government under which he lived could not interfere to prevent a sacrifice? Or if a wife religiously believed it was her duty to burn herself upon the funeral pile of her dead husband, would it be beyond the power of the civil government to prevent her carrying her belief into practice?

So here, as a law of the organization of society under the exclusive dominion of the United States, it is provided that plural marriages shall not be allowed. Can a man excuse his practices to the contrary because of his religious belief? To permit this would be to make the professed doctrines of religious belief superior to the law of the land, and in effect to permit every citizen to become a law unto himself. Government could exist only in name under such circumstances.

A criminal intent is generally an element of crime, but every man is presumed to intend the necessary and legitimate consequences of what he knowingly does. Here the accused knew he had been once married, and that his first wife was living. He also knew that his second marriage was forbidden by law. When, therefore, he married the second time, he is presumed to have intended to break the law. And the breaking of the law is the crime. Every act necessary to constitute the crime was knowingly done, and the crime was therefore knowingly committed. Ignorance of effect may sometimes be taken as evidence of a want of criminal intent, but not ignorance of the law. The only defence of the accused in this case is his belief that the law ought not to have been enacted. It matters not that his belief was a part of his professed religion: it was still belief, and belief only.

In *Regina v. Wagstaff* (10 Cox Crim. Cases, 531), the parents of a sick child, who omitted to call in medical attendance because of their religious belief that what they did for its cure would be effective, were held not to be guilty of manslaughter, while it was said the contrary would have been the result if the child had actually been starved to death by the parents, under the notion that it was their religious duty to abstain from giving it food. But when the offence consists of a positive act which is knowingly done, it would be dangerous to hold that the offender might escape punishment because he religiously believed the law which he had broken ought never to have been made. No case, we believe, can be found that has gone so far.

Upon a careful consideration of the whole case, we are satisfied that no error was committed by the court below.

Judgment affirmed.

EMPLOYMENT DIVISION v. SMITH
494 U.S. 872 (1990)

JUSTICE SCALIA delivered the opinion of the Court.

This case requires us to decide whether the Free Exercise Clause of the First Amendment permits the State of Oregon to include religiously inspired peyote use within the reach of its general criminal prohibition on use of that drug, and thus permits the State to deny unemployment benefits to persons dismissed from their jobs because of such religiously inspired use.

Oregon law prohibits the knowing or intentional possession of a "controlled substance" unless the substance has been prescribed by a medical practitioner. Ore.Rev.Stat. §475.992(4) (1987). The law defines "controlled substance" as a drug classified in Schedules I through V of the Federal Controlled Substances Act, 21 U.S.C. §§811–812 (1982 ed. and Supp. V), as modified by the State Board of Pharmacy. Ore.Rev.Stat. §475.005(6) (1987). Persons who violate this provision by possessing a controlled substance listed on Schedule I are "guilty of a Class B felony." §475.992(4)(a). As compiled by the State Board of Pharmacy under its statutory authority, see Ore.Rev.Stat. §475.035 (1987),

Schedule I contains the drug peyote, a hallucinogen derived from the plant *Lophophorawilliamsii Lemaire*. Ore.Admin. Rule 855–80–021(3)(s) (1988).

Respondents Alfred Smith and Galen Black were fired from their jobs with a private drug rehabilitation organization because they ingested peyote for sacramental purposes at a ceremony of the Native American Church, of which both are members. When respondents applied to petitioner Employment Division for unemployment compensation, they were determined to be ineligible for benefits because they had been discharged for work-related "misconduct." The Oregon Court of Appeals reversed that determination, holding that the denial of benefits violated respondents' free exercise rights under the First Amendment.

On appeal to the Oregon Supreme Court, petitioner argued that the denial of benefits was permissible because respondents' consumption of peyote was a crime under Oregon law. The Oregon Supreme Court reasoned, however, that the criminality of respondents' peyote use was irrelevant to resolution of their constitutional claim—since the purpose of the "misconduct" provision under which respondents had been disqualified was not to enforce the State's criminal laws but to preserve the financial integrity of the compensation fund, and since that purpose was inadequate to justify the burden that disqualification imposed on respondents' religious practice. . . .

Before this Court in 1987, petitioner continued to maintain that the illegality of respondents' peyote consumption was relevant to their constitutional claim. We agreed, concluding that "if a State has prohibited through its criminal laws certain kinds of religiously motivated conduct without violating the First Amendment, it certainly follows that it may impose the lesser burden of denying unemployment compensation benefits to persons who engage in that conduct." We noted, however, that the Oregon Supreme Court had not decided whether respondents' sacramental use of peyote was in fact proscribed by Oregon's controlled substance law, and that this issue was a matter of dispute between the parties. Being "uncertain about the legality of the religious use of peyote in Oregon," we determined that it would not be "appropriate for us to decide whether the practice is protected by the Federal Constitution." . . . Accordingly, we vacated the judgment of the Oregon Supreme Court and remanded for further proceedings.

On remand, the Oregon Supreme Court held that respondents' religiously inspired use of peyote fell within the prohibition of the Oregon statute, which "makes no exception for the sacramental use" of the drug. . . . It then considered whether that prohibition was valid under the Free Exercise Clause, and concluded that it was not. The court therefore reaffirmed its previous ruling that the State could not deny unemployment benefits to respondents for having engaged in that practice. . . .

The Free Exercise Clause of the First Amendment, which has been made applicable to the States by incorporation into the Fourteenth Amendment, see *Cantwell v. Connecticut*, 310 U.S. 296, 303 (1940), provides that "Congress shall make no law respecting an establishment of religion, or *prohibiting the free exercise thereof . . .*" U.S. Const. Am. I (emphasis added). The free exercise of religion means, first and foremost, the right to believe and profess whatever religious doctrine one desires. Thus, the First Amendment obviously excludes all "governmental regulation of religious *beliefs* as such." . . .

But the "exercise of religion" often involves not only belief and profession but the performance of (or abstention from) physical acts: assembling with others for a worship service, participating in sacramental use of bread and wine, proselytizing, abstaining from certain foods or certain modes of transportation. It would be true, we think (though no case of ours has involved the point), that a state would be "prohibiting the free exercise [of religion]" if it sought to ban such acts or abstentions only when they are engaged in for religious reasons, or only because of the religious belief that they display. It would doubtless be unconstitutional, for example, to ban the casting of "statues that are to be used for worship purposes," or to prohibit bowing down before a golden calf.

Respondents in the present case, however, seek to carry the meaning of "prohibiting the free exercise [of religion]" one large step further. They contend that their religious motivation for using peyote places them beyond the reach of a criminal law that is not specifically directed at their religious practice, and that is concededly constitutional as applied to those who use the drug for other reasons. They assert, in other words, that "prohibiting the free exercise [of religion]" includes requiring any individual to observe a generally applicable law that requires (or forbids) the performance of an act that his religious belief forbids (or requires). As a textual matter, we do not think the words must be given that meaning. It is no more necessary to regard the collection of a general tax, for example, as "prohibiting the free exercise [of religion]" by those citizens who believe support of organized government to be sinful, than it is to regard the same tax as "abridging the freedom . . . of the press" of those publishing companies that must pay the tax as a condition of staying in business. It is a permissible reading of the text, in the one case as in the other, to say that if prohibiting the exercise of religion (or burdening the activity of printing) is not the object of the tax but merely the incidental effect of a generally applicable and otherwise valid provision, the First Amendment has not been offended. . . .

We have never held that an individual's religious beliefs excuse him from compliance with an otherwise valid law prohibiting conduct that the State is free to regulate. On the contrary, the record of more than a century of our free exercise jurisprudence contradicts that proposition. As described succinctly by Justice Frankfurter in *Minersville School District v. Gobitis*, 310 U.S. 586, 594–595 (1940): "Conscientious scruples have not, in the course of the long struggle for religious toleration, relieved the individual from obedience to a general law not aimed at the promotion or restriction of religious beliefs. The mere possession of religious convictions which contradict the relevant concerns of a political society does not relieve the citizen from the discharge of political responsibilities (footnote omitted)." We first had occasion to assert that principle in *Reynolds v. United States*, 98 U.S. 145 (1879), where we rejected the claim that criminal laws against polygamy could not be constitutionally applied to those whose religion commanded the practice. "Laws," we said, "are made for the government of actions, and while they cannot interfere with mere religious belief and opinions, they may with practices. . . . Can a man excuse his practices to the contrary because of his religious belief? To permit this would be to make the professed doctrines of religious belief superior to the law of the land, and in effect to permit every citizen to become a law unto himself." *Id.*, at 166–167.

Subsequent decisions have consistently held that the right of free exercise does not relieve an individual of the obligation to comply with a "valid and neutral law of general applicability on the ground that the law proscribes (or prescribes) conduct that his religion prescribes (or proscribes)." *United States v. Lee*, 455 U.S. 252, 263, n. 3 (1982) (Stevens, J., concurring in judgment); see *Minersville School Dist. Bd. of Educ. v. Gobitis, supra*, at 595 (collecting cases). In *Prince v. Massachusetts*, 321 U.S. 158 (1944), we held that a mother could be prosecuted under the child labor laws for using her children to dispense literature in the streets, her religious motivation notwithstanding. We found no constitutional infirmity in "excluding [these children] from doing there what no other children may do." *Id.*, at 171. In *Braunfeld v. Brown*, 366 U.S. 599 (1961) (plurality opinion), we upheld Sunday-closing laws against the claim that they burdened the religious practices of persons whose religions compelled them to refrain from work on other days. In *Gillette v. United States*, 401 U.S. 437, 461 (1971), we sustained the military selective service system against the claim that it violated free exercise by conscripting persons who opposed a particular war on religious grounds. . . .

The only decisions in which we have held that the First Amendment bars application of a neutral, generally applicable law to religiously motivated action have involved not the Free Exercise Clause alone, but the Free Exercise Clause in conjunction with other constitutional protections, such as freedom of speech and of the press, see *Cantwell v. Connecticut*, 310 U.S., at 304–307 (invalidating a licensing system for religious and charitable solicitations under which the administrator had discretion to deny a license to any cause he deemed nonreligious); *Murdock v. Pennsylvania*, 319 U.S. 105 (1943) (invalidating a flat tax on solicitation as applied to the dissemination of religious ideas); *Follett v. McCormick*, 321 U.S. 573 (1944) (same), or the right of parents, acknowledged in *Pierce v. Society of Sisters*, 268 U.S. 510 (1925), to direct the education of their children, see *Wisconsin v. Yoder*, 406 U.S. 205 (1972) (invalidating compulsory school-attendance laws as applied to Amish parents who refused on religious grounds to send their children to school). Some of our cases prohibiting compelled expression, decided exclusively upon free speech grounds, have also involved freedom of religion, cf. *Wooley v. Maynard*, 430 U.S. 705 (1977) (invalidating compelled display of a license plate slogan that offended individual religious beliefs); *West Virginia Board of Education v. Barnette*, 319 U.S. 624 (1943) (invalidating compulsory flag salute statute challenged by religious objectors).

The present case does not present such a hybrid situation, but a free exercise claim unconnected with any communicative activity or parental right. Respondents urge us to hold, quite simply, that when otherwise prohibitable conduct is accompanied by religious convictions, not only the convictions but the conduct itself must be free from governmental regulation. We have never held that, and decline to do so now. There being no contention that Oregon's drug law represents an attempt to regulate religious beliefs, the communication of religious beliefs, or the raising of one's children in those beliefs, the rule to which we have adhered ever since *Reynolds* plainly controls. . . .

Respondents argue that even though exemption from generally applicable criminal laws need not automatically be extended to religiously motivated actors, at least the claim for a religious exemption must be evaluated under the balancing test set forth in *Sherbert v. Verner*, 374 U.S. 398 (1963). Under the *Sherbert* test, governmental actions that substantially burden a religious practice must be justified by a compelling governmental interest. . . . Applying that test we have, on three occasions, invalidated state unemployment compensation rules that conditioned the availability of benefits upon an applicant's willingness to work under conditions forbidden by his religion. . . . We have never invalidated any governmental action on the basis of the *Sherbert* test except the denial of unemployment compensation. Although we have sometimes purported to apply the *Sherbert* test in contexts other than that, we have always found the test satisfied, see *United States v. Lee*, 455 U.S. 252 (1982); *Gillette v. United States*, 401 U.S. 437 (1971). In recent years we have abstained from applying the *Sherbert* test (outside the unemployment compensation field) at all. In *Bowen v. Roy*, 476 U.S. 693 (1986), we declined to apply *Sherbert* analysis to a federal statutory scheme that required benefit applicants and recipients to provide their Social Security numbers. The plaintiffs in that case asserted that it would violate their religious beliefs to obtain and provide a Social Security number for their daughter. We held the statute's application to the plaintiffs valid regardless of whether it was necessary to effectuate a compelling interest. See *id.*, at 699–701. In *Lyng v. Northwest Indian Cemetery Protective Assn.*, 485 U.S. 439 (1988), we declined to apply *Sherbert* analysis to the Government's logging and road construction activities on lands used for religious purposes by several Native American Tribes, even though it was undisputed that the activities "could have devastating effects on traditional Indian religious practices," 485 U.S., at 451. In *Goldman v. Weinberger*, 475 U.S. 503 (1986), we rejected application of the *Sherbert* test to military dress regulations that forbade the wearing of yarmulkes. In *O'Lone v. Estate of Shabazz*, 482 U.S. 342 (1987), we sustained, without mentioning the *Sherbert* test, a prison's refusal to excuse inmates from work requirements to attend worship services.

Even if we were inclined to breathe into *Sherbert* some life beyond the unemployment compensation field, we would not apply it to require exemptions from a generally applicable criminal law. The *Sherbert* test, it must be recalled, was developed in a context that lent itself to individualized governmental assessment of the reasons for the relevant conduct. As a plurality of the Court noted in *Roy*, a distinctive feature of unemployment compensation progams is that their eligibility criteria invite consideration of the particular circumstances behind an applicant's unemployment: "The statutory conditions [in *Sherbert* and *Thomas*] provided that a person was not eligible for unemployment compensation benefits if, 'without good cause,' he had quit work or refused available work. The 'good cause' standard created a mechanism for individualized exemptions." . . . As the plurality pointed out in *Roy*, our decisions in the unemployment cases stand for the proposition that where the State has in place a system of individual exemptions, it may not refuse to extend that system to cases of "religious hardship" without compelling reason. *Bowen v. Roy, supra,* at 708.

Whether or not the decisions are that limited, they at least have nothing to do with an across-the-board criminal prohibition on a particular form of conduct. Although, as noted earlier, we have sometimes used the *Sherbert* test to analyze free exercise challenges to such laws, . . . we have never applied the test to invalidate one. We conclude today that the sounder approach, and the approach in accord with the vast majority of our precedents, is to hold the test inapplicable to such challenges. The government's ability to enforce generally applicable prohibitions of socially harmful conduct, like its ability to carry out other aspects of public policy, "cannot depend on measuring the effects of a governmental action on a religious objector's spiritual development." *Lyng, supra,* at 451. To make an individual's obligation to obey such a law contingent upon the law's coincidence with his religious beliefs, except where the State's interest is "compelling"—permitting him, by virtue of his beliefs, "to become a law unto himself," *Reynolds v. United States*, 98 U.S., at 167—contradicts both constitutional tradition and common sense.

The "compelling government interest" requirement seems benign, because it is familiar from other fields. But using it as the standard that must be met before the government may accord different treatment on the basis of race, see, *e.g.*, *Palmore v. Sidoti*, 466 U.S. 429, 432 (1984), or before the government may regulate the content of speech, see, *e.g.*, *Sable Communications of California v. FCC*, 492 U.S. 115, 126 (1989), is not remotely comparable to using it for the purpose asserted here. What it produces in those other fields—equality of treatment, and an unrestricted flow of contending speech—are constitutional norms; what it would produce here—a private right to ignore generally applicable laws—is a constitutional anomaly.

Nor is it possible to limit the impact of respondents' proposal by requiring a "compelling state interest" only when the conduct prohibited is "central" to the individual's religion. . . . It is no more appropriate for judges to determine the "centrality" of religious beliefs before applying a "compelling interest" test in the free exercise field, than it would be for them to determine the "importance" of ideas before applying the "compelling interest" test in the free speech field. What principle of law or logic can be brought to bear to contradict a believer's assertion that a particular act is "central" to his personal faith? Judging the centrality of different religious practices is akin to the unacceptable "business of evaluating the relative merits of differing religious claims." *United States v. Lee*, 455 U.S., at 263 n. 2 (Stevens, J., concurring). As we reaffirmed only last Term, "[i]t is not within the judicial ken to question the centrality of particular beliefs or practices to a faith, or the validity of particular litigants' interpretation of those creeds." *Hernandez v. Commissioner*, 490 U.S., at 699. Repeatedly and in many different contexts, we have warned that courts must not presume to determine the place of a particular belief in a religion or the plausibility of a religious claim. . . .

If the "compelling interest" test is to be applied at all, then, it must be applied across the board, to all actions thought to be religiously commanded. Moreover, if "compelling interest" really means what it says (and watering it down here would subvert its rigor in the other fields where it is applied), many laws will not meet the test. Any society adopting such a system would be courting anarchy, but that danger increases in direct proportion to the society's diversity of religious beliefs, and its determination to coerce or suppress none of them. Precisely because "we are a cosmopolitan nation made up of people of almost every conceivable religious preference," *Braunfeld v. Brown*, 366 U.S., at 606, and precisely because we value and protect that religious divergence, we cannot afford the luxury of deeming *presumptively invalid*, as applied to the religious objector, every regulation of conduct that does not protect an interest of the highest order. . . .

Because respondents' ingestion of peyote was prohibited under Oregon law, and because that prohibition is constitutional, Oregon may, consistent with the Free Exercise Clause, deny respondents unemployment compensation when their dismissal results from use of the drug. The decision of the Oregon Supreme Court is accordingly reversed.

It is so ordered.

Concurring Opinion JUSTICE O'CONNOR, with whom JUSTICE BRENNAN, JUSTICE MARSHALL, and JUSTICE BLACKMUN join as to Parts I and II, concurring in the judgment.

Although I agree with the result the Court reaches in this case, I cannot join its opinion. In my view, today's holding dramatically departs from well-settled First Amendment jurisprudence, appears unnecessary to resolve the question presented, and is incompatible with our Nation's fundamental commitment to individual religious liberty. . . .

The Court today extracts from our long history of free exercise precedents the single categorical rule that "if prohibiting the exercise of religion . . . is . . . merely the incidental effect of a generally applicable and otherwise valid provision, the First Amendment has not been offended." . . . Indeed, the Court holds that where the law is a generally applicable criminal prohibition, our usual free exercise jurisprudence does not even apply. . . . To reach this sweeping result, however, the Court must not only give a strained reading of the First Amendment but must also disregard our consistent application of free exercise doctrine to cases involving generally applicable regulations that burden religious conduct. . . .

The Court today, however, interprets the Clause to permit the government to prohibit, without justification, conduct mandated by an individual's religious beliefs, so long as that prohibition is generally applicable. . . . But a law that prohibits certain conduct—conduct that happens to be an act of worship for someone—manifestly does prohibit that person's free exercise of his religion. A person who is barred from engaging in religiously motivated conduct is barred from freely exercising his religion. Moreover, that person is barred from freely exercising his religion regardless of whether the law prohibits the conduct only when engaged in for religious reasons, only by members of that religion, or by all persons. It is difficult to deny that a law that prohibits religiously motivated conduct, even if the law is generally applicable, does not at least implicate First Amendment concerns. . . .

To say that a person's right to free exercise has been burdened, of course, does not mean that he has an absolute right to engage in the conduct. Under our established First Amendment jurisprudence, we have recognized that the freedom to act, unlike the freedom to believe, cannot be absolute. See, *e.g.*, *Cantwell, supra*, 310 U.S., at 304; *Reynolds v. United States*, 98 U.S. 145, 161–167 (1879). Instead, we have respected both the First Amendment's express textual mandate and the governmental interest in regulation of conduct by requiring the Government to justify any substantial burden on religiously motivated conduct by a compelling state interest and by means narrowly tailored to achieve that interest. . . .

Respondents, of course, do not contend that their conduct is automatically immune from all governmental regulation simply because it is motivated by their sincere religious beliefs. The Court's rejection of that argument . . . might therefore be regarded as merely harmless dictum. Rather, respondents invoke our traditional compelling interest test to argue that the Free Exercise Clause requires the State to grant them a limited exemption from its general criminal prohibition against the possession of peyote. The Court today, however, denies them even the opportunity to make that argument, concluding that "the sounder approach, and the approach in accord with the vast majority of our precedents, is to hold the [compelling interest] test inapplicable to" challenges to general criminal prohibitions. . . .

Legislatures, of course, have always been "left free to reach actions which were in violation of social duties or subversive of good order." *Reynolds*, 98 U.S., at 164; see also *Yoder*, 406 U.S., at 219–220; *Braunfeld*, 366 U.S., at 603–604. Yet because of the close relationship between conduct and religious belief, "[i]n every case the power to regulate must be so exercised as not, in attaining a permissible end, unduly to infringe the protected freedom."*Cantwell*, 310 U.S., at 304. Once it has been shown that a government regulation or criminal prohibition burdens the free exercise of religion, we have consistently asked the Government to demonstrate that unbending application of its regulation to the religious objector "is essential to accomplish an overriding governmental interest," *Lee, supra*, at 257–258, or represents "the least restrictive means of achieving some compelling state interest," *Thomas, supra*, 450 U.S., at 718. . . . To me, the sounder approach—the approach more consistent with our role as judges to decide each case on its individual merits—is to apply this test in each case to determine whether the burden on the specific plaintiffs before us is constitutionally significant and whether the particular criminal interest asserted by the State before us is compelling. Even if, as an empirical matter, a government's criminal laws might usually serve a compelling interest in health, safety, or public order, the First Amendment at least requires a case-by-case determination of the question, sensitive to the facts of each particular claim. . . .

I would therefore adhere to our established free exercise jurisprudence and hold that the State in this case has a compelling interest in regulating peyote use by its citizens and that accommodating respondents' religiously motivated conduct "will unduly interfere with fulfillment of the governmental interest."

Dissenting Opinion JUSTICE BLACKMUN, with whom JUSTICE BRENNAN and JUSTICE MARSHALL join, dissenting.

This Court over the years painstakingly has developed a consistent and exacting standard to test the constitutionality of a state statute that burdens the free exercise of religion. Such a statute may stand only if the law in general, and the State's refusal to allow a religious exemption in particular, are justified by a compelling interest that cannot be served by less restrictive means. . . .

In weighing respondents' clear interest in the free exercise of their religion against Oregon's asserted interest in enforcing its drug laws, it is important to articulate in precise terms the state interest involved. It is not the State's broad interest in fighting the critical "war on drugs" that must be weighed against respondents' claim, but the State's narrow interest in refusing to make an exception for the religious, ceremonial use of peyote. . . .

The State proclaims an interest in protecting the health and safety of its citizens from the dangers of unlawful drugs. It offers, however, no evidence that the religious use of peyote has ever harmed anyone. The factual findings of other courts cast doubt on the State's assumption that religious use of peyote is harmful. . . .

The fact that peyote is classified as a Schedule I controlled substance does not, by itself, show that any and all uses of peyote, in any circumstance, are inherently harmful and dangerous. . . .

The carefully circumscribed ritual context in which respondents used peyote is far removed from the irresponsible and unrestricted recreational use of unlawful drugs. The Native American Church's internal restrictions on, and supervision of, its members' use of peyote substantially obviate the State's health and safety concerns. . . .

Finally, the State argues that granting an exception for religious peyote use would erode its interest in the uniform, fair, and certain enforcement of its drug laws. The State fears that, if it grants an exemption for religious peyote use, a flood of other claims to religious exemptions will follow. It would then be placed in a dilemma, it says, between allowing a patchwork of exemptions that would hinder its law enforcement efforts, and risking a violation of the Establishment Clause by arbitrarily limiting its religious exemptions. This argument, however, could be made in almost any free exercise case. See Lupu, Where Rights Begin: The Problem of Burdens on the Free Exercise of Religion, 102 Harv.L.Rev. 933, 947 (1989) ("Behind every free exercise claim is a spectral march; grant this one, a voice whispers to each judge, and you will be confronted with an endless chain of exemption demands from religious deviants of every stripe"). This Court, however, consistently has rejected similar arguments in past free exercise cases, and it should do so here as well. . . .

The State's apprehension of a flood of other religious claims is purely speculative. Almost half the States, and the Federal Government, have maintained an exemption for religious peyote use for many years, and apparently have not found themselves overwhelmed by claims to other religious exemptions. Allowing an exemption for religious peyote use would not necessarily oblige the State to grant a similar exemption to other religious groups. The unusual circumstances that make the religious use of peyote compatible with the State's interests in health and safety and in preventing drug trafficking would not apply to other religious claims. Some religions, for example, might not restrict drug use to a limited ceremonial context, as does the Native American Church. See, *e.g.*, *Olsen*, 279 U.S.App.D.C., at 7, 878 F.2d, at 1464 ("the Ethiopian Zion Coptic Church . . . teaches that marijuana is properly smoked 'continually all day' "). Some religious claims, see n. 8, *supra*, involve drugs such as marijuana and heroin, in which there is significant illegal traffic, with its attendant greed and violence, so that it would be difficult to grant a religious exception without seriously compromising law enforcement efforts. That the State might grant an exemption for religious peyote use, but deny other religious claims arising in different circumstances, would not violate the Establishment Clause. Though the State must treat all religions equally, and not favor one over another, this obligation is fulfilled by the uniform application of the "compelling interest" *test* to all free exercise claims, not by reaching uniform *results* as to all claims. A showing that religious peyote use does not unduly interfere with the State's interests is "one that probably few other religious groups or sects could make," *Yoder*, 406 U.S., at 236; this does not mean that an exemption limited to peyote use is tantamount to an establishment of religion. . . .

Respondents believe, and their sincerity has *never* been at issue, that the peyote plant embodies their deity, and eating it is an act of worship and communion. Without peyote, they could not enact the essential ritual of their religion. . . .

If Oregon can constitutionally prosecute them for this act of worship, they, like the Amish, may be "forced to migrate to some other and more tolerant region." *Yoder*, 406 U.S., at 218. This potentially devastating impact must be viewed in light of the federal policy—reached in reaction to many years of religious persecution and intolerance—of protecting the religious freedom of Native Americans. . . .

For these reasons, I conclude that Oregon's interest in enforcing its drug laws against religious use of peyote is not sufficiently compelling to outweigh respondents' right to the free exercise of their religion. Since the State could not constitutionally enforce its criminal prohibition against respondents, the interests underlying the State's drug laws cannot justify its denial of unemployment benefits. Absent such justification, the State's regulatory interest in denying benefits for religiously motivated "misconduct," . . . is indistinguishable from the state interests this Court has rejected in *Frazee*, *Hobbie*, *Thomas*, and *Sherbert*. The State of Oregon cannot, consistently with the Free Exercise Clause, deny respondents unemployment benefits.

I dissent.

················· DISCUSSION QUESTIONS ·················

1. Do you agree with the Court's decision in *Employment Division v. Smith*? Do you agree with a majority of the justices that if the Court cannot imagine where a line would be drawn between acceptable and unacceptable violations of criminal laws by religious people, then it should not even try? If the Court had begun to draw lines between acceptable and unacceptable behavior, might it have found that task to be easier than first thought?

2. Both the *Reynolds* and *Smith* cases involved what are commonly called "victimless" crimes. Do you agree that polygamy and drug use are "victimless"? If these decisions had been in favor of the defendants, would that have made it impossible for government to enforce most laws regarding "victimless" crimes because people charged with violating these laws would simply say that their religion made them do it?

3. It appears from the decision in the *Ballard* case that people are free to make any claims about strictly "religious" matters when asking for money. Apparently people can promise to pray for other people or to intercede with saints or with God regardless of whether or not they can fulfill these promises. If after people sent money to someone to pray for them, it could be proven that prayers were never made, could the person who promised to pray then be sent to jail? Could the people who sent money sue to get their money back?

4. The author suggests that if the religious cannot be kept from ringing doorbells or passing out literature, then other groups such as political groups also cannot be kept from such activity. Do you agree? If only the religious had this right, would that violate the Establishment Clause?

5. Some people have argued that if the authors of the First Amendment had intended to only protect belief and speech, they would not have used the words "free exercise" of religion. These people argue that the word "exercise" implies action, the use of the body and so on. What do you think of this argument?

6. The right to freely exercise religion does not include the right to have a human sacrifice. Does it include the right to tell people that human sacrifice is a good thing?

7. What if a person who was to be the victim of human sacrifice wanted to be sacrificed? Should that make a difference? What if the person killed himself or herself while others watched and did nothing to stop the suicide? Would it be within the power of the state to prosecute those observers for not stopping the person from committing suicide?

8. Justice Scalia said in *Employment Division v. Smith* that it is impossible for judges to decide whether a belief is "central" to a person's religion. If this is true, how can judges make decisions in conscientious objector cases?

CHAPTER
eight
The Wall of Separation Today

When examining the complex area of separation of church and state, people often overlook the fact that there is much the members of the Court have agreed on. In the first modern-era Supreme Court case concerned with the Establishment Clause, *Everson v. Board of Education* (see p. 44), Justice Black summarized his interpretation of the meaning of the Establishment Clause (see p. 36), outlining what the government may not do. Members of the Court have been able to agree with this interpretation as well as with Thomas Jefferson's statement that there must be a "wall of separation between church and state."

At the same time, a majority of the members of the Court have consistently believed that governments can accommodate religion in many situations. They have held that too high a wall of separation between church and state sends a message that government disapproves of religion, and the Court should not force the government to send this message.

In the decisions discussed in chapters 2, 3, and 4, the Court tried to interpret the meaning of the Establishment Clause. Reciting prayers in public schools violated the Establishment Clause, the Court decided, because prayer in public schools sends a message of governmental endorsement of religion, and impressionable schoolchildren are likely to conclude that only the type of religion endorsed by government is correct. The members of the Court believed this also interfered with the right of parents to train their children in matters of religion, free from government interference. At the same time, a majority of the justices did not think that they had to go to the logical extreme in this area. Allowing invocations to open legislative sessions did not, in the opinion of the Court, fall into the same category as prayer in public schools.

When dealing with the use of religious symbols by government, the Court decided that some recognition of the religious nature of the country is permissible, as long as it does not go too far in sending a message of "endorsement" of religion in general or of a particular religion. A nativity scene as part of a large Christmas display is acceptable, but the same scene standing alone in the middle of a courthouse is not.

The most difficult cases in the area of the separation of church and state have been concerned with the extent to which government may provide support for private religious schools below the college level. Again, the Court has refused to take the easy way out and outlaw all support, no matter how small or indirect. Instead, the Court has spent several decades trying to define what is acceptable government support and what is not. At present, tuition reimbursements and tax credits are not acceptable, but tax deductions for expenditures by parents who send their children to religious schools are acceptable. While many people have criticized the Court's decisions on this issue, there is no perfect solution. At any point good arguments can be made that too much or too little government support is being allowed.

In the area of protecting the right to freely exercise religion, the Court has been forced over the course of half a century to explore more fully what the general right of free speech protects and includes. The Court has come to the conclusion that the Free Exercise Clause protects the right not to speak, as well as the right to speak. Thus, children may not be expelled from school for refusing to say the Pledge of Allegiance to the flag. The Free Exercise Clause protects the right to speak in public parks, to go door-to-door passing out literature and selling books, and to collect money for religious purposes without unreasonable regulation by government.

The rights of religious freedom and free speech also include the right to learn and to get an education. What good is the right to speak if people do not understand what they are saying or hearing? Government may not have a monopoly over education; parents and students must be free to seek out knowledge wherever they believe it to be.

The right of religious freedom does not include the right to break the criminal law, however. The Court concluded in 1878, and again in 1990, that to rule otherwise would create a whole new set of problems for the Court and for society. It would require courts to try to determine the central beliefs of a religion, and to weigh those beliefs against the importance of the goals legislatures were trying to achieve by passing particular statutes. It would also place the Court in the position of establishing religion by granting to the religious a privilege denied to the rest of the citizenry. This would appear as an endorsement of religion and might encourage people to join a religious sect simply to avail themselves of these privileges. This is clearly something the Court must avoid doing.

Arguments have been made that the Court could determine the kinds of laws that the right of religious freedom overrides and the kinds of laws that cannot be overridden. The problem is that every member of the Court is aware of how difficult this kind of line drawing has turned out to be in the area of government support for religious schools. There is no reason to believe that the process would be any easier in the case of criminal laws.

Over the decades, the justices have had a great deal of difficulty interpreting the Establishment and Free Exercise clauses and communicating their reasons for voting one way or another. Justices Black and Douglas voted to allow states to pay for the bus transportation of children to religious schools, but they both felt very strongly that providing textbooks on nonreligious subjects to these same students violated the First Amendment. The distinction they were trying to make was lost on the other members of the Court. What is the difference between paying for a bus and paying for a book? Both forms of support aid religious schools, have nothing to do with religion, and could be seen as gifts to the students and their parents rather than as aid to religious schools.

We discussed in Chapter 1 the fact that in this area of constitutional decision making the Court is constantly on the horns of a dilemma. If the Court moves too far to allow religious freedom, it risks violating the Establishment Clause. If the Court moves too far to outlaw government support of religion, it risks violating the Free Exercise Clause.

There is one decision discussed in this book where it could be argued that the Court did go too far. That decision is *Wisconsin v. Yoder* (see p. 105). In that decision Chief Justice Burger allowed parents who were members of a particular religious sect to violate the compulsory education laws in order to keep their children out of high school. In doing so, he made the point that only religions of long standing would be allowed to violate the law in this way. To grant this privilege only to a few religious sects and to deny it to everyone else discriminates between different religions. New religions will not be allowed this privilege. In most of its other decisions over half a century, the Court has been careful to avoid taking the age or character of a religion into account. The *Yoder* decision also gives a privilege to the religious that is denied to the nonreligious. In all the other Court decisions concerned with religious freedom, the same rights given to religious people to believe and speak also applied to others who wished to discuss or believe something nonreligious.

The rest of the decisions discussed in this book logically follow from one another and avoid, for the most part, getting hung up on either horn of the religion dilemma. While citizens can disagree with any particular Court conclusion, the Supreme Court is applying a consistent logic to these cases that can be applied by other courts throughout the country.

Even taking *Yoder* into account, people in the United States have a pretty good idea of where the wall of separation between church and state is in the 1990s, how high it is, and what falls on either side. While anyone can disagree with the exact location and configuration of the wall, it seems to have accomplished its purpose. The United States has more religious diversity than any other country on earth and has been able to avoid religious conflict. The government has not been weakened because of its identification or lack of identification with religion in general or with particular religions. Most of the concerns of philosophers such as John Locke and Baron de Montesquieu have been addressed, and most of the goals of men such as Thomas Jefferson and James Madison have been met. Most people in the United States do not believe that they suffer under a great deal of pressure from government to change their religious beliefs or practices, and most do not feel they can no longer support the government of the United States because of their religious beliefs.

We must never forget that unlike the other parts of the Bill of Rights, the First Amendment contains rights the founders of the new nation believed were of the greatest importance if democracy was to survive. They believed that democracy could not survive without free speech, a free press, and the freedom to assemble. They also believed democracy would suffer if religion and government were not kept separate.

The Supreme Court and American society have learned over two centuries that absolute religious freedom, in the sense of freedom to do whatever one's religion demands, is simply not possible. Other nations have been able to allow one group to have complete religious freedom only by making that religion the established church and outlawing or limiting the rights of all other religions. That is an option the United States has never realistically had. From the time of the American Revolution to the present, a great diversity of religious beliefs has characterized the makeup of the American population, and no one religious group could have claimed to represent the majority of Americans.

As the United States prepares to enter a new century, it is as important to look back as it is to look forward. Americans tend to focus on what divides society, and the issues discussed in this book have certainly been potentially divisive. The Supreme Court has been aware of this, and has tried to steer a middle course between the various views on these issues. Looking back, it seems that the Court has been, in the main, successful. There is a wall of separation between the church and the state. It is not as straight nor as tall as it might have been, but it is certainly taller and straighter than the authors of the First Amendment had any right to expect it to be. After all, no society on earth had tried to maintain order and government without an established church. It was and still is part of what is a unique experiment in democracy and freedom that is the United States of America.

GLOSSARY OF
LEGAL TERMS

● ● ● ● ● ● ● ● ●

A *fortiori*: Latin, meaning literally "from the stronger." It is used by judges to mean that if one fact exists, another fact must follow from it. If someone is alive, then we know *a fortiori* that he or she is breathing.

Allegation: A statement of fact that has not yet been proven. In a criminal case we would say that allegations have been made against the defendant which the prosecutor will attempt to prove.

Amicus curiae: Latin, meaning literally "a friend of the Court." In some cases, especially in cases that have been appealed, other people besides those people directly involved in a case may have an interest in the outcome. In an effort to influence the justices, these people will file briefs as "friends of the Court," suggesting why the decision should come out one way or the other. When people file *amicus curiae* briefs, they are usually arguing that the court's decision will have an impact on them or on society in general which the court should consider when making its decision.

Analogy: A way of thinking about an issue that relates a particular situation to another situation by identifying similarities. People involved in a case often argue that their case is analogous (or similar) to another case because they know what the court decided in the other case and they would like the court to make the same decision in their case.

Appeal: A request to a higher court to review the decision of a lower court. When a trial is over, the losing party may appeal the decision to an appeals court.

Appellant/Appellee: The appellant is the person who appeals a case to a higher court; the appellee is the person who has to respond to the appeal.

Atheist: A person who does not believe in the existence of a God.

Bill of attainder: A law passed by a legislature declaring that a particular person or a group of persons is guilty of a crime. The person, or group of persons, to whom the bill of attainder applies has not received a trial.

Brief: A written document given to a judge to support a particular legal opinion. When a case is appealed to a higher court, each side will file a brief explaining why it should win the case. Other people may also file briefs as "friends of the Court" (*amicus curiae* briefs), pointing out the effects a decision may have on them or on society in general.

Certiorari: Latin, meaning literally "to be certain." In American law, when someone wants to appeal his or her case to the U.S. Supreme Court, he or she usually asks for a writ of certiorari. If the Court agrees to hear the case, it issues a writ of certiorari which orders the parties in the case to bring the case before the court.

Circuit Court of Appeals: In the federal judicial system, the district court conducts the trial and the Supreme Court hears cases on appeal. There is an appeals court between the district court and the Supreme Court, called the circuit court. Generally a case must be appealed to the circuit court before it can go on to the Supreme Court.

Citizen: Someone who is a full legal member of a nation. In the United States, only a citizen can vote and hold some public offices.

Civil: In American law, most cases are either civil or criminal. In a civil case, one person sues another person. In a criminal case, the government claims that someone has broken the law and should pay a fine or go to jail.

Common law: Common law is law made by judges as opposed to statutes passed by legislatures. In ancient times, people were subject to the laws of their tribe. After his conquest of England in 1066 A.D., William I decided that there should be one law for all of the subjects in his kingdom. This law was developed mainly by the king's judges, as they made decisions and then based later decisions on their decisions in earlier cases. Over the centuries the English judges developed many legal principles that became the basis for most of their decisions in civil cases. These principles became the common law for England and her colonies. The United States inherited this common law. It has been modified by the judges in each state over the centuries, so that today each state is considered to have its own unique common law. The main exception to this is Louisiana, which bases its law on French and Spanish law, not the English common law.

Conscientious objector: A person who, for reasons of conscience, objects to fighting in a war. To qualify as a true "conscientious objector," the person must believe that war is objectionable in general, and not just object to a particular war.

Constitution: In the United States, the Constitution is a written document that forms the supreme law and organization of the government. Governments may exercise only those powers granted to them by the Constitution and they are limited by the rights reserved for the individual citizens.

Criminal: *See* **Civil.**

De minimis: The short form of the Latin phrase *de minimis non curat lex,* which means the law does not care about very "minimal" or small things. If a legal violation is technically a violation of the law but so small as to be not worth the court's time, the judge may dismiss the case as *de minimis.*

Defendant: A defendant is someone who is being sued or is charged with committing a crime.

Dicta: From the Latin, meaning statements of opinion by a judge that are not directly relevant to the decision of the case. Dicta are general statements concerning a particular judge's definition of the law but that do not directly relate to the case before the court.

Dissent: When a group of judges is making a decision and some of the judges do not agree with the majority, they will "dissent" from the majority opinion. To dissent simply means to disagree. They may state their dissent, or they may write a dissenting opinion explaining why they disagree. On some occasions a dissenting opinion has convinced the group to reverse its opinion about a decision.

District court: In the federal judicial system, trial of a case is held at the district court. A case may then be appealed to the circuit court, and from there to the Supreme Court. It is the district court that determines the facts of the case.

Ex post facto law: A law passed after an act has been committed. Conviction on the basis of an ex post facto law is not allowed in the United States; a person may only be convicted of acts for which laws were actually on the books when the act was committed.

Holding: The decision of the court and the reason for that decision. Attorneys generally say that the holding of the case is the reason why the winning party in a case was successful.

Impeachment: Impeachment occurs when a public official is removed from office for having done something illegal or immoral.

In loco parentis: Latin, meaning literally "in the place of the parent." *In loco parentis* is a legal concept that says that if someone, such as a babysitter or a teacher, has been put in charge of a child, then that person has the same power over the child that the child's parent would have.

Infra: Latin, meaning literally "below." If a judge mentions a case briefly that he or she will be discussing in detail later in the decision, then the judge may put the word *infra* after the name of the case. This lets the reader know that the case will be discussed later in more detail.

Injunction: A court order telling a person to do, or not to do, something. People might say that a person has been "injoined" from acting. A restraining order is one kind of injunction.

Interstate commerce: The movement of goods across state lines in the United States. Under the U.S. Constitution, the federal government is given the power to control "interstate commerce" to make sure that goods flow between states with a minimum of disruption.

Jurisdiction: The area over which a particular court has power. For example, the U.S. Supreme Court can only decide cases concerned with federal law and questions of constitutional interpretation. Most issues are within the jurisdiction of state courts, not federal courts.

Mens rea: Latin, meaning literally "guilty mind." Generally, a person cannot be found guilty of a crime unless he or she had a "guilty mind," meaning he or she intended to do harm or to commit a crime.

Naturalization: The process by which a noncitizen becomes a citizen.

Parens patriae: Latin, meaning literally "the parent of the country." In ancient times this term meant that the king was regarded as the ultimate parent for everyone and had the power to act as the parent of any subject in the kingdom if the subject's real parents were not available. In countries without a king, the term means that, if there is no natural parent to deal with a problem, then the government may have to fulfill that function. For example, the government may act as a parent in dealing with a child, with an insane person, or with someone who is not capable of dealing with things for himself or herself.

Per curiam: Latin, meaning literally "by the court." When an opinion has been written by the court as a whole, rather than by one particular judge, it is called a *per curiam* decision.

Petitioner: A person who petitions a judge to make a decision. Someone who files a lawsuit or begins an appeal can be called a petitioner. The person who is being sued or is defending against an appeal is the respondent.

Plaintiff: In a lawsuit, the person who brings the lawsuit is called the plaintiff. The person being sued by the plaintiff is called the defendant. The defendant defends against the charges that have been brought by the plaintiff.

Police power: A concept of U.S. law. Courts in the United States have decided that state constitutions provide state governments with police power, meaning the power to do everything that it is "reasonable" for government to do. Although the U.S. Constitution spells out the powers of the federal government, most state constitutions do not do this. The police power is very broad and includes the power to build roads, fight disease, and put people in jail; however, a court can decide that a particular action by a state legislature is unconstitutional if it is beyond the police power. The problem with this broad concept is that it is very vague and gives courts a great deal of power to declare the actions of legislatures to be unconstitutional as a violation of the state constitution. If a state government takes action beyond its power, the court does not have to ask whether or not any rights protected by the Bill of Rights have been violated. A court may invalidate an action of government either because the action was beyond the power of government or because it violated a right protected by the Bill of Rights.

Precedent: In the U.S. legal system, lower courts are bound by the decisions of courts above them. We say that those higher court decisions serve as precedents for the decisions to be made by the lower courts.

Restraining order: A court order that orders someone not to do something. If a person wants to stop another person from doing something, he or she may ask a judge for a restraining order against that other person.

Scienter: Latin, meaning "knowingly." Generally people cannot be convicted of crimes unless they acted knowingly, with scienter, meaning that the people knew what they were doing when they committed the crime. They were not acting unconsciously or without knowledge of the facts in the case.

Separation of powers: Generally government is thought of as having three basic powers: the power to make the law (legislative), the power to enforce the law (executive), and the power to decide what the law is (judicial). In the United States, these three powers are separate from each other. That has not always been true in other countries or in the past. In ancient Athens, for example, the legislature was also the supreme court.

Standing: In the American legal system, people are generally not allowed to complain about the violation of the law or the Constitution unless the violation has injured them personally in some way. Only people who actually have been injured have standing to complain about their injury either in a civil or criminal case.

Stare decisis: Latin, meaning literally "the decision must stand." In American law, once a particular court has made a decision, it is expected that the court will not change its ruling. People can then alter their behavior to comply with the decision without fear that it will change in the near future. This concept is particularly important for the U.S. Supreme Court because Supreme Court decisions have such a far-reaching impact on society.

Statute: A law passed by a legislative body, such as a state legislature or the U.S. Congress.

Stipulate: The purpose of a trial is to determine the facts of a particular case. If there are facts on which both sides agree, then both sides will "stipulate" that those facts are true and correct. For the rest of the trial, everyone will assume that those facts are true without having to prove them.

Supra: Latin, meaning literally "above." If a judge has already discussed a case in detail and wishes to mention it briefly again, he or she may put the word *supra* after the name of the case to let the reader know that the case has already been discussed in detail earlier in the decision.

Tort: Comes from the same Latin root as words such as *twist* and *torture*. In American law, if one person has injured another person in some way, we say that a tort has been committed. The injury may be physical, economic, or psychological. When people sue because they have been injured, we say they are "suing in tort."

Ubiquity: The concept that something can be everywhere at the same time, omnipresent. Some believe that God is ubiquitous. We generally conceive that the law and government are ubiquitous, even if there is no government official at a particular place at a particular time.

Writ of habeas corpus: A court order that requires a person who has someone in or under custody to either bring that person to court or release him or her from custody.

FURTHER READING

Carter, Stephen L. *The Culture of Disbelief*. New York: Basic Books, 1993.
Discusses the relationship between the American government and legal system and religion.

Davis, Derek. *Original Intent*. Buffalo, NY: Prometheus Books, 1991.
Examines Chief Justice Rehnquist's impact on the debate about the proper separation between church and state in the United States and is generally critical of the chief justice's attempt to search for the original intent of the authors of the First Amendment.

Dolbeare, Kenneth, and Hammond, Phillip E. *The School Prayer Decisions*. Chicago: The University of Chicago Press, 1971.
Examines a community that continued to say prayers in the public schools for many years after the Supreme Court declared the practice unconstitutional.

Edel, Wilbur. *Defenders of the Faith*. New York: Praeger, 1987.
Examines the evolution of the relationship between religion and law in the United States.

Goldberg, George. *Church, State and the Constitution*. Washington, DC: Regnery Gateway, 1987.
Criticizes Supreme Court decisions in the area of religion and argues in favor of prayer in the public schools.

Hunter, James Davison, and Guinness, Os, eds. *Articles of Faith, Articles of Peace*. Washington, DC: The Brookings Institution, 1990.
A collection of essays on religious freedom in the United States.

Kleeberg, Irene Cumming. *Separation of Church and State*. New York: F. Watts, 1986.
Examines the issue of the separation of church and state in the United States in a way that is intended to be accessible to younger children.

Lauback, John Herbert. *School Prayers*. Washington, DC: Public Affairs Press, 1969.
> Examines the reaction by the public and Congress to the Supreme Court's decision to outlaw prayer in public schools.

Levy, Leonard W. *The Establishment Clause*. New York: Macmillan Publishing Co., 1986.
> Examines the interpretation of the Establishment Clause of the First Amendment through two centuries of American history.

Maddox, Robert L. *Separation of Church and State*. New York: The Crossroad Publishing Co., 1987.
> Argues that the only way to maintain religious freedom is to maintain the separation of church and state.

Manwaring, David R. *Render unto Caesar*. Chicago: The University of Chicago Press, 1962.
> Examines the history of the Supreme Court's decisions concerning the Pledge of Allegiance to the American flag in public school and the impact of those decisions on American society.

Morgan, Richard E. *The Supreme Court and Religion*. New York: The Free Press, 1972.
> Examines the evolution of the Supreme Court's thinking about religion over the course of several decades.

Reichley, A. James. *Religion in American Public Life*. Washington, DC: The Brookings Institution, 1985.
> Examines the history of the relationship between religion and politics in the United States.

Rice, Charles E. *The Supreme Court and Public Prayer*. New York: Fordham University Press, 1964.
> Argues that prayers should be allowed in public schools.

Smith, Rodney K. *Public Prayer and the Constitution*. Wilmington, DE: Scholarly Resources, Inc., 1987.
> Examines the evolution of the Supreme Court's decisions on the issue of prayer in public places such as schools and legislatures.

Stevens, Leonard A. *Salute! The Case of the Bible vs. the Flag*. New York: Coward, McCann & Geoghegan, 1973.
> Examines the evolution of the Supreme Court's decisions concerning the Pledge of Allegiance to the American flag in a way that is intended to be accessible to younger children.

Stokes, Anson Phelps, and Pfeffer, Leo. *Church and State in the United States*. Westport, CT: Greenwood Press, 1964.
Generally considered to be the classic philosophical treatise on the subject of church and state relations in the United States.

Swanson, Wayne R. *The Christ Child Goes to Court*. Philadelphia: Temple University Press, 1990.
Examines the history and effect of the Supreme Court's decision in *Lynch v. Donnelly* concerning the placing of nativity scenes on public property in Rhode Island.

Wald, Kenneth D. *Religion and Politics in the United States*. New York: St. Martin's Press, 1987.
Examines the history of the relationships between religion, politics, and law in the United States.

APPENDIX A

•••••••••

Constitution of the United States

PREAMBLE

We the People of the United States, in Order to form a more perfect Union, establish Justice, insure domestic Tranquility, provide for the common defence, promote the general Welfare, and secure the Blessings of Liberty to ourselves and our Posterity, do ordain and establish this Constitution for the United States of America.

ARTICLE I

Section 1. All legislative Powers herein granted shall be vested in a Congress of the United States, which shall consist of a Senate and House of Representatives.

Section 2. The House of Representatives shall be composed of Members chosen every second Year by the People of the several States, and the Electors in each State shall have the Qualifications requisite for Electors of the most numerous Branch of the State Legislature.

No Person shall be a Representative who shall not have attained to the age of twenty five Years, and been seven Years a Citizen of the United States, and who shall not, when elected, be an Inhabitant of that State in which he shall be chosen.

Representatives and direct Taxes shall be apportioned among the several States which may be included within this Union, according to their respective Numbers, which shall be determined by adding to the whole Number of free Persons, including those bound to Service for a Term of Years, and excluding Indians not taxed, three fifths of all other Persons. The actual Enumeration shall be made within three Years after the first Meeting of the Congress of the

United States, and within every subsequent Term of ten Years, in such Manner as they shall by Law direct. The Number of Representatives shall not exceed one for every thirty Thousand, but each State shall have at Least one Representative; and until such enumeration shall be made, the State of New Hampshire shall be entitled to chuse three, Massachusetts eight, Rhode-Island and Providence Plantations one, Connecticut five, New-York six, New Jersey four, Pennsylvania eight, Delaware one, Maryland six, Virginia ten, North Carolina five, South Carolina five, and Georgia three.

When vacancies happen in the Representation from any State, the Executive Authority thereof shall issue Writs of Election to fill such Vacancies.

The House of Representatives shall chuse their Speaker and other Officers; and shall have the sole Power of Impeachment.

Section 3. The Senate of the United States shall be composed of two Senators from each State, chosen by the Legislature thereof, for six Years; and each Senator shall have one Vote.

Immediately after they shall be assembled in Consequence of the first Election, they shall be divided as equally as may be into three Classes. The Seats of the Senators of the first Class shall be vacated at the Expiration of the second Year, of the second Class at the Expiration of the fourth Year, and of the third Class at the Expiration of the sixth Year, so that one third may be chosen every second Year; and if Vacancies happen by Resignation, or otherwise, during the Recess of the Legislature of any State the Executive thereof may make temporary Appointments until the next Meeting of the Legislature, which shall then fill such Vacancies.

No Person shall be a Senator who shall not have attained to the Age of thirty Years, and been nine Years a Citizen of the United States, and who shall not, when elected, be an Inhabitant of that State for which he shall be chosen.

The Vice President of the United States shall be President of the Senate, but shall have no Vote, unless they be equally divided.

The Senate shall chuse their other Officers, and also a President pro tempore, in the Absence of the Vice President, or when he shall exercise the Office of President of the United States.

The Senate shall have the sole Power to try all Impeachments. When sitting for that Purpose, they shall be on Oath or Affirmation. When the President of the United States is tried the Chief Justice shall preside: And no Person shall be convicted without the Concurrence of two thirds of the Members present.

Judgment in Cases of Impeachment shall not extend further than to removal from Office, and disqualification to hold and enjoy any Office of honor, Trust or Profit under the United States: but the Party convicted shall nevertheless be liable and subject to Indictment, Trial, Judgment and Punishment, according to Law.

Section 4. The Times, Places and Manner of holding Elections for Senators and Representatives, shall be prescribed in each State by the Legislature thereof; but the Congress may at any time by Law make or alter such Regulations, except as to the Places of chusing Senators.

The Congress shall assemble at least once in every Year, and such Meeting shall be on the first Monday in December, unless they shall by Law appoint a different Day.

Section 5. Each House shall be the Judge of the Elections, Returns and Qualifications of its own Members, and a Majority of each shall constitute a Quorum to do Business; but a smaller Number may adjourn from day to day, and may be authorized to compel the Attendance of absent Members, in such Manner, and under such Penalties as each House may provide.

Each House may determine the Rules of its Proceedings, punish its Members for disorderly Behaviour, and, with the Concurrence of two thirds, expel a Member.

Each House shall keep a Journal of its Proceedings, and from time to time publish the same, excepting such Parts as may in their Judgment require Secrecy; and the Yeas and Nays of the Members of either House on any question shall, at the Desire of one fifth of those Present, be entered on the Journal.

Neither House, during the Session of Congress, shall, without the Consent of the other, adjourn for more than three days, nor to any other Place than that in which the two Houses shall be sitting.

Section 6. The Senators and Representatives shall receive a Compensation for their Services, to be ascertained by Law, and paid out of the Treasury of the United States. They shall in all Cases, except Treason, Felony and Breach of the Peace, be privileged from Arrest during their Attendance at the Session of their respective Houses, and in going to and returning from the same; and for any Speech or Debate in either House, they shall not be questioned in any other Place.

No Senator or Representative shall, during the Time for which he was elected, be appointed to any civil Office under the Authority of the United States, which shall have been created, or the Emoluments whereof shall have been encreased during such time; and no Person holding any Office under the United States, shall be a Member of either House during his Continuance in Office.

Section 7. All Bills of raising Revenue shall originate in the House of Representatives; but the Senate may propose or concur with amendments as on other Bills.

Every Bill which shall have passed the House of Representatives and the Senate, shall, before it become a Law, be presented to the President of the United States; If he approve he shall sign it, but if not he shall return it, with his Objections to that House in which it shall have originated, who shall enter the Objections at large on their Journal, and proceed to reconsider it. If after such Reconsideration two thirds of that House shall agree to pass the Bill, it shall be sent, together with the Objections, to the other House, by which it shall likewise be reconsidered, and if approved by two thirds of that House, it shall become a Law. But in all such Cases the Votes of both Houses shall be determined by yeas and Nays, and the Names of the Persons voting for and against the Bill shall be entered on the Journal of each House respectively. If any Bill shall not be returned by the President within ten Days (Sunday excepted) after it shall have been presented to him, the Same shall be a Law, in like Manner as if he had signed it, unless the Congress by their Adjournment prevent its Return, in which Case it shall not be a Law.

Every Order, Resolution, or Vote to which the Concurrence of the Senate and House of Representatives may be necessary (except on a question of Adjournment) shall be presented to the President of the United States; and before the Same shall take Effect, shall be approved by him, or being disapproved by him, shall be repassed by two thirds of the Senate and House of Representatives, according to the Rules and Limitations prescribed in the Case of a Bill.

Section 8. The Congress shall have Power To lay and collect Taxes, Duties, Imposts and Excises, to pay the Debts and provide for the common Defence and general Welfare of the United States; but all Duties, Imposts and Excises shall be uniform throughout the United States;

To borrow Money on the credit of the United States;

To regulate Commerce with foreign Nations, and among the several States, and with the Indian Tribes;

To establish an uniform Rule of Naturalization, and uniform Laws on the subject of Bankruptcies throughout the United States;

To coin Money, regulate the Value thereof, and of foreign Coin, and fix the Standard of Weights and Measures;

To provide for the Punishment of counterfeiting the Securities and current Coin of the United States;

To establish Post Offices and post Roads;

To promote the Progress of Science and useful Arts, by securing for limited Times to Authors and Inventors the exclusive Right to their respective Writings and Discoveries;

To constitute Tribunals inferior to the supreme Court;

To define and punish Piracies and Felonies commit[t]ed on the high Seas, and Offences against the Law of Nations;

To declare War, grant Letters of Marque and Reprisal, and make Rules concerning Captures on Land and Water;

To raise and support Armies, but no Appropriation of Money to that Use shall be for a longer Term than two Years;

To provide and maintain a Navy;

To make Rules for the Government and Regulation of the land and naval Forces;

To provide for calling forth the Militia to execute the Laws of the Union, suppress Insurrections and repel Invasions;

To provide for organizing, arming, and disciplining the Militia, and for governing such Part of them as may be employed in the Service of the United States, reserving to the States respectively, the Appointment of the Officers, and the Authority of training the Militia according to the discipline prescribed by Congress;

To exercise exclusive Legislation in all Cases whatsoever, over such District (not exceeding ten Miles square) as may, by Cession of Particular States, and the Acceptance of Congress, become the Seat of the Government of the United States, and to exercise like Authority over all Places purchased by the Consent of the Legislature of the State in which the Same shall be, for the Erection of Forts, Magazines, Arsenals, dock-Yards, and other needful Buildings;

—And

To make all Laws which shall be necessary and proper for carrying into Execution the foregoing Powers, and all other Powers vested by this Constitution in the Government of the United States, or in any Department or Officer thereof.

Section 9. The Migration or Importation of such Persons as any of the States now existing shall think proper to admit, shall not be prohibited by the Congress prior to the Year one thousand eight hundred and eight, but a Tax or duty may be imposed on such Importation, not exceeding ten dollars for each Person.

The Privilege of the Writ of Habeas Corpus shall not be suspended, unless when in Cases of Rebellion or Invasion the public Safety may require it.

No Bill of Attainder or ex post facto law shall be passed.

No capitation, or other direct, Tax shall be laid, unless in Proportion to the Census of Enumeration herein before directed to be taken.

No Tax or Duty shall be laid on Articles exported from any State.

No Preference shall be given by any Regulation of Commerce or Revenue to the Ports of one State over those of another; nor shall Vessels bound to, or from, one State, be obliged to enter, clear or pay Duties in another.

No Money shall be drawn from the Treasury, but in Consequence of Appropriations made by Law; and a regular Statement and Account of the Receipts and Expenditures of all public Money shall be published from time to time.

No Title of Nobility shall be granted by the United States: And no Person holding any Office of Profit or Trust under them, shall without the Consent of the Congress, accept of any present, Emolument, Office, or Title, of any kind whatever, from any King, Prince or foreign State.

Section 10. No State shall enter into any Treaty, Alliance, or Confederation; grant Letters of Marque and Reprisal; coin Money; emit Bills of Credit; make any Thing but gold and silver Coin a Tender in Payment of Debts; pass any Bill of Attainder, ex post facto Law, or Law impairing the Obligation of Contracts, or grant any Title of Nobility.

No State shall, without the Consent of the Congress, lay any Imposts or Duties on Imports or Exports, except what may be absolutely necessary for executing it's inspection Laws: and the net Produce of all Duties and Imposts, laid by any State on Imports or Exports, shall be for the Use of the Treasury of the United States; and all such Laws shall be subject to the Revision and Controul of the Congress.

No State shall, without the Consent of Congress, lay any Duty of Tonnage, keep Troops, or Ships of War in time of Peace, enter into any Agreement or Compact with another State, or with a foreign Power, or engage in War, unless actually invaded, or in such imminent Danger as will not admit of delay.

ARTICLE II

Section 1. The executive Power shall be vested in a President of the United States of America. He shall hold his Office during the Term of four Years, and, together with the Vice President, chosen for the same Term, be elected, as follows.

Each State shall appoint, in such Manner as the Legislature thereof may direct, a Number of Electors, equal to the whole Number of Senators and Representatives to which the State may be entitled in the Congress: but no Senator or Representative, or Person holding an Office of Trust or Profit under the United States, shall be appointed an Elector.

The Electors shall meet in their respective States, and vote by Ballot for two Persons, of whom one at least shall not be an Inhabitant of the same State with themselves. And they shall make a List of all the Persons voted for, and of the Number of Votes for each; which List they shall sign and certify, and transmit sealed to the Seat of the Government of the United States, directed to the President of the Senate. The President of the Senate shall, in the Presence of the Senate and House of Representatives, open all the Certificates, and the Votes shall then be counted. The Person having the greatest Number of Votes shall be the President, if such Number be a Majority of the whole Number of Electors appointed; and if there be more than one who have such Majority, and have an equal Number of Votes, then the House of Representatives shall immediately chuse by Ballot one of them for President; and if no Person have a Majority, then from the five highest on the list the said House shall in like Manner chuse the President. But in chusing the President, the Votes shall be taken by States, the Representation from each State having one Vote; a quorum for this Purpose shall consist of a Member or Members from two thirds of the States, and a Majority of all the States shall be necessary to a Choice. In every Case, after the Choice of the President, the Person having the greatest Number of Votes of the Electors shall be the Vice President. But if there should remain two or more who have equal Votes, the Senate shall chuse from them by Ballot the Vice President.

The Congress may determine the Time of chusing the Electors, and the Day on which they shall give their Votes; which Day shall be the same throughout the United States.

No Person except a natural born Citizen, or a Citizen of the United States, at the time of the Adoption of this Constitution, shall be eligible to the Office of President; neither shall any Person be eligible to that Office who shall not have attained to the Age of thirty five Years, and been fourteen Years a Resident within the United States.

In Case of the Removal of the President from Office, or of his Death, Resignation, or Inability to discharge the Powers and Duties of the said Office, the Same shall devolve on the Vice President, and the Congress may by Law provide for the Case of Removal, Death, Resignation or Inability, both of the President and Vice President, declaring what Officer shall then act as President, and such Officer shall act accordingly, until the Disability be removed, or a President shall be elected.

The President shall, at stated Times, receive for his Services, a Compensation, which shall neither be increased nor diminished during the Period for which he shall have been elected, and he shall not receive within that Period any other Emolument from the United States, or any of them.

Before he enter on the Execution of his Office, he shall take the following Oath or Affirmation:—"I do solemnly swear (or affirm) that I will faithfully execute the Office of President of the United States, and will to the best of my Ability, preserve, protect and defend the Constitution of the United States."

Section 2. The President shall be Commander in Chief of the Army and Navy of the United States, and of the Militia of the several States, when called into the actual Service of the United States; he may require the Opinion, in writing, of the principal Officer in each of the executive Departments, upon any Subject relating to the Duties of their respective Offices, and he shall have Power to grant Reprieves and Pardons for Offenses against the United States, except in Cases of Impeachment.

He shall have Power, by and with the Advice and Consent of the Senate, to make Treaties, provided two thirds of the Senators present concur; and he shall nominate, and by and with the Advice and Consent of the Senate, shall appoint Ambassadors, other public Ministers and Consuls, Judges of the supreme Court, and all other Officers of the United States, whose Appointments are not herein otherwise provided for, and which shall be established by Law: but the Congress may by Law vest the Appointment of such inferior Officers, as they think proper, in the President alone, in the Courts of Law, or in the Heads of Departments.

The President shall have Power to fill up all Vacancies that may happen during the Recess of the Senate, by granting Commissions which shall expire at the End of their next Session.

Section 3. He shall from time to time give to the Congress Information of the State of the Union, and recommend to their Consideration such Measures as he shall judge necessary and expedient; he may, on extraordinary Occasions, convene both Houses, or either of them, and in Case of Disagreement between them, with Respect to the Time of Adjournment, he may adjourn them to such Time as he shall think proper; he shall receive Ambassadors and other public Ministers; he shall take Care that the Laws be faithfully executed, and shall Commission all the Officers of the United States.

Section 4. The President, Vice President and all Civil Officers of the United States, shall be removed from office on Impeachment for, and Conviction of, Treason, Bribery, or other high Crimes and Misdemeanors.

ARTICLE III

Section 1. The judicial Power of the United States shall be vested in one supreme Court, and in such inferior Courts as the Congress may from time to time ordain and establish. The Judges, both of the supreme and inferior Courts, shall hold their Offices during good Behaviour, and shall, at stated Times, receive for their Services, a Compensation, which shall not be diminished during their Continuance in Office.

Section 2. The judicial Power shall extend to all Cases, in Law and Equity, arising under this Constitution, the Laws of the United States, and Treaties made, or which shall be made, under their Authority;—to all Cases affecting Ambassadors, other public Ministers and Consuls;—to all Cases of admiralty and maritime Jurisdiction;—to Controversies to which the United States shall be a Party;—to Controversies between two or more States;—between a State and Citizens of another State;—between Citizens of different States;—between Citizens of the same State claiming Lands under Grants of different States, and between a State, or the Citizens thereof, and foreign States, Citizens or Subjects.

In all Cases affecting Ambassadors, other public Ministers and Consuls, and those in which a State shall be Party, the supreme Court shall have original Jurisdiction. In all the other Cases before mentioned, the supreme Court shall have appellate Jurisdiction, both as to Law and Fact, with such Exceptions, and under such Regulations as the Congress shall make.

The Trial of all Crimes, except in cases of Impeachment, shall be by Jury; and such Trial shall be held in the State where the said Crimes shall have been committed; but when not committed within any State, the Trial shall be at such Place or Places as the Congress may by Law have directed.

Section 3. Treason against the United States shall consist only in levying War against them, or in adhering to their Enemies, giving them Aid and Comfort. No Person shall be convicted of Treason unless on the Testimony of two Witnesses to the same overt Act, or on Confession in open Court.

The Congress shall have Power to declare the Punishment of Treason, but no Attainder of Treason shall work Corruption of Blood, or Forfeiture except during the Life of the Person attainted.

ARTICLE IV

Section 1. Full Faith and Credit shall be given in each State to the public Acts, Records, and judicial Proceedings of every other State. And the Congress may by general Laws prescribe the Manner in which such Acts, Records and Proceedings shall be proved, and the Effect thereof.

Section 2. The Citizens of each State shall be entitled to all Privileges and Immunities of Citizens in the several States.

A Person charged in any State with Treason, Felony, or other Crime, who shall flee from Justice, and be found in another State, shall on Demand of the executive Authority of the State from which he fled, be delivered up, to be removed to the State having Jurisdiction of the Crime.

No Person held to Service or Labour in one State, under the Laws thereof, escaping into another, shall, in Consequence of any Law or Regulation therein, be discharged from such Service or Labour, but shall be delivered up on Claim of the Party to whom such Service or Labour may be due.

Section 3. New States may be admitted by the Congress into this Union; but no new State shall be formed or erected within the Jurisdiction of any other State; nor any State be formed by the Junction of two or more States, or Parts of States, without the Consent of the Legislatures of the States concerned as well as of the Congress.

The Congress shall have Power to dispose of and make all needful Rules and Regulations respecting the Territory or other Property belonging to the United States; and nothing in this Constitution shall be so construed as to Prejudice any Claims of the United States, or of any particular State.

Section 4. The United States shall guarantee to every State in this Union a Republican Form of Government, and shall protect each of them against invasion; and on Application of the Legislature, or of the Executive (when the Legislature cannot be convened) against domestic Violence.

ARTICLE V

The Congress, whenever two thirds of both Houses shall deem it necessary, shall propose Amendments to this Constitution, or, on the Application of the Legislatures of two thirds of the several States, shall call a Convention for proposing Amendments, which, in either Case, shall be valid to all Intents and Purposes, as Part of this Constitution, when ratified by the Legislatures of three fourths of the several States, or by Conventions in three fourths thereof, as the one or the other Mode of Ratification may be proposed by the Congress; Provided that no Amendment which may be made prior to the Year One thousand eight hundred and eight shall in any Manner affect the first and fourth Clauses in the Ninth Section of the first Article; and that no State, without its Consent, shall be deprived of its equal Suffrage in the Senate.

ARTICLE VI

All Debts contracted and Engagements entered into, before the Adoption of this Constitution, shall be as valid against the United States under this Constitution, as under the Confederation.

This Constitution, and the Laws of the United States which shall be made in Pursuance thereof; and all Treaties made, or which shall be made, under the Authority of the United States, shall be the supreme Law of the Land; and the Judges in every State shall be the supreme Law of the Land; and the Judges in every State shall be bound thereby, any Thing in the Constitution or Laws or any State to the Contrary notwithstanding.

The Senators and Representatives before mentioned, and the Members of the several State Legislatures, and all executive and judicial Officers, both of the United States and of the several States, shall be bound by Oath or Affirmation, to support this Constitution; but no religious Test shall ever be required as a Qualification to any Office or public Trust under the United States.

ARTICLE VII

The Ratification of the Conventions of nine States, shall be sufficient for the Establishment of this Constitution between the States so ratifying the Same.

AMENDMENTS

Amendment I

Congress shall make no law respecting an establishment of religion, or prohibiting the free exercise thereof; or abridging the freedom of speech, or of the press; or the right of the people peaceably to assemble, and to petition the Government for a redress of grievances.

Amendment II

A well regulated Militia, being necessary to the security of a free State, the right of the people to keep and bear Arms, shall not be infringed.

Amendment III

No Soldier shall, in time of peace be quartered in any house, without the consent of the Owner, nor in time of war, but in a manner to be prescribed by law.

Amendment IV

The right of the people to be secure in their persons, houses, papers, and effects, against unreasonable searches and seizures, shall not be violated, and no Warrants shall issue, but upon probable cause, supported by Oath or affirmation, and particularly describing the place to be searched, and the persons or things to be seized.

Amendment V

No person shall be held to answer for a capital, or otherwise infamous crime, unless on a presentment or indictment of a Grand Jury, except in cases arising in the land or naval forces, or in the Militia, when in actual service in time of War or public danger; nor shall any person be subject for the same offence to be twice put in jeopardy of life or limb; nor shall be compelled in any criminal case to be a witness against himself, nor be deprived of life, liberty, or property, without due process of law; nor shall private property be taken for public use, without just compensation.

Amendment VI

In all criminal prosecutions, the accused shall enjoy the right to a speedy and public trial, by an impartial jury of the State and district wherein the crime shall have been committed, which district shall have been previously ascertained by law, and to be informed of the nature and cause of the accusation; to be confronted with the witnesses against him; to have compulsory process for obtaining witnesses in his favor, and to have the Assistance of Counsel for his defence.

Amendment VII

In Suits at common law, where the value in controversy shall exceed twenty dollars, the right of trial by jury shall be preserved, and no fact tried by a jury, shall be otherwise reexamined in any Court of the United States, than according to the rules of the common law.

Amendment VIII

Excessive bail shall not be required, nor excessive fines imposed, nor cruel and unusual punishments inflicted.

Amendment IX

The enumeration in the Constitution, of certain rights, shall not be construed to deny or disparage others retained by the people.

Amendment X

The powers not delegated to the United States by the Constitution, nor prohibited by it to the States, are reserved to the States respectively, or to the people.

[First 10 amendments ratified 15 December 1791]

Amendment XI

The Judicial power of the United States shall not be construed to extend to any suit in law or equity, commenced or prosecuted against one of the United States by Citizens of another State, or by Citizens or Subjects of any Foreign State.

[Ratified 7 February 1795]

Amendment XII

The Electors shall meet in their respective states and vote by ballot for President and Vice-President, one of whom, at least, shall not be an inhabitant of the same state with themselves; they shall name in their ballots the person voted for as President, and in distinct ballots the person voted for as Vice-President, and they shall make distinct lists of all persons voted for as President, and of all persons voted for as Vice-President, and of the number of votes for each, which lists they shall sign and certify, and transmit sealed to the seat of the government of the United States, directed to the President of the Senate;—The President of the Senate shall, in the presence of the Senate and House of Representatives, open all the certificates and the votes shall then be counted;—The person having the greatest number of votes for President, shall be the President, if such number be a majority of the whole number of Electors appointed; and if no person have such majority, then from the persons having the highest numbers not exceeding three on the list of those voted for as President, the House of Representatives shall chuse immediately, by ballot, the President. But in chusing the President, the votes shall be taken by states, the representation from each state having one vote; a quorum for this purpose shall consist of a member or members from two-thirds of the states, and a majority of all the states shall be necessary to a choice. And if the House of Representatives shall not chuse a President whenever the right of choice shall devolve upon them, before the fourth day of March next following, then the Vice-President shall act as President, as in the case of the death or other constitutional disability of the President—The person having the greatest number of votes as Vice-President, shall be the Vice-President, if such number be a majority of the whole number of Electors appointed, and if no person have a majority, then from the two highest numbers on the list, the Senate shall chuse the Vice-President; a quorum for the purpose shall consist of two-thirds of the whole number of Senators, and a majority of the whole number shall be necessary to a choice. But no person constitutionally ineligible to the office of President shall be eligible to that of Vice-President of the United States.

[Ratified 15 June 1804]

Amendment XIII

Section 1. Neither slavery nor involuntary servitude, except as a punishment for crime whereof the party shall have been duly convicted, shall exist within the United States, or any place subject to their jurisdiction.

Section 2. Congress shall have power to enforce this article by appropriate legislation.

[Ratified 6 December 1865]

Amendment XIV

Section 1. All persons born or naturalized in the United States and subject to the jurisdiction thereof, are citizens of the United States and of the State wherein they reside. No State shall make or enforce any law which shall abridge the privileges or immunities of citizens of the United States; nor shall any State deprive any person of life, liberty, or property, without due process of law; nor deny to any person within its jurisdiction the equal protection of the laws.

Section 2. Representatives shall be apportioned among the several States according to their respective numbers, counting the whole number of persons in each State, excluding Indians not taxed. But when the right to vote at any election for the choice of electors for President and Vice President of the United States, Representatives in Congress, the Executive and Judicial officers of a State, or the members of the Legislature thereof, is denied to any of the male inhabitants of such State, being twenty-one years of age, and citizens of the United States, or in any way abridged, except for participation in rebellion, or other crime, the basis of representation therein shall be reduced in the proportion which the number of such male citizens shall bear to the whole number of male citizens twenty-one years of age in such State.

Section 3. No person shall be a Senator or Representative in Congress, or elector of President and Vice President, or hold any office, civil or military, under the United States, or under any State, who, having previously taken an oath, as a member of Congress, or as an officer of the United States, or as a member of any State legislature, or as an executive or judicial officer of any State, to support the Constitution of the United States, shall have engaged in insurrection or rebellion against the same, or given aid or comfort to the enemies thereof. But Congress may by a vote of two-thirds of each House, remove such disability.

Section 4. The validity of the public debt of the United States, authorized by law, including debts incurred for payment of pensions and bounties for services in suppressing insurrection or rebellion, shall not be questioned. But neither the United States nor any State shall assume or pay any debt or obligation incurred in aid of insurrection or rebellion against the United States, or any claim for the loss or emancipation of any slave; but all such debts, obligations and claims shall be held illegal and void.

Section 5. The Congress shall have power to enforce, by appropriate legislation, the provisions of this article.

[Ratified 9 July 1868]

Amendment XV

Section 1. The right of citizens of the United States to vote shall not be denied or abridged by the United States or by any State on account of race, color, or previous condition of servitude.

Section 2. The Congress shall have power to enforce this article by appropriate legislation.

[Ratified 3 February 1870]

Amendment XVI

The Congress shall have power to lay and collect taxes on incomes, from whatever source derived, without apportionment among the several States, and without regard to any census or enumeration.

[Ratified 3 February 1913]

Amendment XVII

The Senate of the United States shall be composed of two Senators from each State, elected by the people thereof, for six years; and each Senator shall have one vote. The electors in each State shall have the qualifications requisite for electors of the most numerous branch of the State legislatures.

When vacancies happen in the representation of any State in the Senate, the executive authority of such State shall issue writs of election to fill such vacancies: *Provided,* That the legislature of any State may empower the executive thereof to make temporary appointments until the people fill the vacancies by election as the legislature may direct.

This amendment shall not be so construed as to affect the election or term of any Senator chosen before it becomes valid as part of the Constitution.

[Ratified 8 April 1913]

Amendment XVIII

Section 1. After one year from the ratification of this article the manufacture, sale, or transportation of intoxicating liquors within, the importation thereof into, or the exportation thereof from the United States and all territory subject to the jurisdiction thereof for beverage purposes is hereby prohibited.

Section 2. The Congress and the several States shall have concurrent power to enforce this article by appropriate legislation.

Section 3. This article shall be inoperative unless it shall have been ratified as an amendment to the Constitution by the legislatures of the several States, as provided in the Constitution, within seven years from the date of the submission hereof to the States by the Congress.

[Ratified 16 January 1919]

Amendment XIX

The right of citizens of the United States to vote shall not be denied or abridged by the United States or by any State on account of sex.

Congress shall have power to enforce this article by appropriate legislation.

[Ratified 18 August 1920]

Amendment XX

Section 1. The terms of the President and Vice President shall end at noon on the 20th day of January, and the terms of Senators and Representatives at noon on the 3d day of January, of the years in which such terms would have ended if this article had not been ratified; and the terms of their successors shall then begin

Section 2. The Congress shall assemble at least once in every year, and such meeting shall begin at noon on the 3d day of January, unless they shall by law appoint a different day.

Section 3. If, at the time fixed for the beginning of the term of the President, the President elect shall have died, the Vice President elect shall become President. If a President shall not have been chosen before the time fixed for the beginning of his term, or if the President elect shall have failed to qualify, then the Vice President elect shall act as President until a President shall have qualified; and the Congress may by law provide for the case wherein neither a President elect nor a Vice President elect shall have qualified, declaring who shall then act as President, or the manner in which one who is to act shall be selected, and such person shall act accordingly until a President or Vice President shall have qualified.

Section 4. The Congress may by law provide for the case of the death of any of the persons from whom the House of Representatives may choose a President whenever the right of choice shall have devolved upon them, and for the case of the death of any of the persons from whom the Senate may choose a Vice President whenever the right of choice shall have devolved upon them.

Section 5. Sections 1 and 2 shall take effect on the 15th day of October following the ratification of this article.

Section 6. This article shall be inoperative unless it shall have been ratified as an amendment to the Constitution by the legislatures of three-fourths of the several States within seven years from the date of its submission.

[Ratified 23 January 1933]

Amendment XXI

Section 1. The eighteenth article of amendment to the Constitution of the United States is hereby repealed.

Section 2. The transportation or importation into any State, Territory or possession of the United States for delivery or use therein of intoxicating liquors, in violation of the laws thereof, is hereby prohibited.

Section 3. This article shall be inoperative unless it shall have been ratified as an amendment to the Constitution by conventions in the several States, as provided in the Constitution, within seven years from the date of the submission hereof to the States by the Congress.

[Ratified 5 December 1933]

Amendment XXII

Section 1. No person shall be elected to the office of the President more than twice, and no person who has held the office of President, or acted as President, for more than two years of a term to which some other person was elected President shall be elected to the office of the President more than once. But this article shall not apply to any person holding the office of President when this Article was proposed by the Congress, and shall not prevent any person who may be holding the office of President, or acting as President, during the term within which this Article become[s] operative from holding the office of President or acting as President during the remainder of such term.

Section 2. This Article shall be inoperative unless it shall have been ratified as an amendment to the Constitution by the legislatures of three-fourths of the several States within seven years from the date of its submission to the States by the Congress.

[Ratified 27 February 1951]

Amendment XXIII

Section 1. The District constituting the seat of Government of the United States shall appoint in such manner as the Congress may direct:

A number of electors of President and Vice President equal to the whole number of Senators and Representatives in Congress to which the District would be entitled if it were a State, but in no event more than the least populous State; they shall be in addition to those appointed by the States, but they shall be considered, for the purposes of the election of President and Vice President, to be electors appointed by a State; and they shall meet in the District and perform such duties as provided by the twelfth article of amendment.

Section 2. The Congress shall have power to enforce this article by appropriate legislation.

[Ratified 29 March 1961]

Amendment XXIV

Section 1. The right of citizens of the United States to vote in any primary or other election for President or Vice President, for electors for President or Vice President, or for Senator or Representative in Congress, shall not be denied or abridged by the United States or any State by reason of failure to pay any poll tax or other tax.

Section 2. The Congress shall have power to enforce this article by appropriate legislation.

[Ratified 23 January 1964]

Amendment XXV

Section 1. In case of the removal of the President from office or of his death or resignation, the Vice President shall become President.

Section 2. Whenever there is a vacancy in the office of the Vice President, the President shall nominate a Vice President who shall take office upon confirmation by a majority vote of both Houses of Congress.

Section 3. Whenever the President transmits to the President pro tempore of the Senate and the Speaker of the House of Representatives his written declaration that he is unable to discharge the powers and duties of his office, and until he transmits to them a written declaration to the contrary, such powers and duties shall be discharged by the Vice President as Acting President.

Section 4. Whenever the Vice President and a majority of either the principal officers of the executive departments or of such other body as Congress may by law provide, transmit to the President pro tempore of the Senate and the Speaker of the House of Representatives their written declaration that the President is unable to discharge the powers and duties of his office, the Vice President shall immediately assume the powers and duties of the office as Acting President.

Thereafter, when the President transmits to the President pro tempore of the Senate and the Speaker of the House of Representatives his written declaration that no inability exists, he shall resume the powers and duties of his office unless the Vice President and a majority of either the principal officers of the executive department or of such other body as Congress may by law provide, transmit within four days to the President pro tempore of the Senate and the Speaker of the House of Representatives their written declaration that the President is unable to discharge the powers and duties of his office. Thereupon Congress shall decide the issue, assembling within forty-eight hours for that purpose if not in session. If the Congress, within twenty-one days after receipt of the latter written declaration, or, if Congress is not in session, within twenty-one days after Congress is required to assemble, determines by two-thirds vote of both houses that the President is unable to discharge the powers and duties of his office, the Vice President shall continue to discharge the same as Acting President; otherwise, the President shall resume the powers and duties of his office.

[Ratified 10 February 1967]

Amendment XXVI

Section 1. The right of citizens of the United States, who are eighteen years of age or older, to vote shall not be denied or abridged by the United States or by any State on account of age.

Section 2. The Congress shall have power to enforce this article by appropriate legislation.

[Ratified 1 July 1971]

Amendment XXVII

No law, varying the compensation for the services of the Senators and Representatives, shall take effect, until an election of Representatives shall have intervened.

[Ratified 7 May 1992]

APPENDIX
B
·········
Justices of the Supreme Court

	Tenure	Appointed by	Replaced
JOHN JAY	1789–1795	Washington	
John Rutledge	1789–1791	Washington	
William Cushing	1789–1810	Washington	
James Wilson	1789–1798	Washington	
John Blair	1789–1796	Washington	
James Iredell	1790–1799	Washington	
Thomas Johnson	1791–1793	Washington	Rutledge
William Paterson	1793–1806	Washington	Johnson
JOHN RUTLEDGE	1795	Washington	Jay
Samuel Chase	1796–1811	Washington	Blair
OLIVER ELLSWORTH	1796–1800	Washington	Rutledge
Bushrod Washington	1798–1829	John Adams	Wilson
Alfred Moore	1799–1804	John Adams	Iredell
JOHN MARSHALL	1801–1835	John Adams	Ellsworth
William Johnson	1804–1834	Jefferson	Moore
Brockholst Livingston	1806–1823	Jefferson	Paterson
Thomas Todd	1807–1826	Jefferson	(new judgeship)
Gabriel Duval	1811–1835	Madison	Chase
Joseph Story	1811–1845	Madison	Cushing
Smith Thompson	1823–1843	Monroe	Livingston

Chief justices' names appear in capital letters.

	Tenure	Appointed by	Replaced
Robert Trimble	1826–1828	John Q. Adams	Todd
John McLean	1829–1861	Jackson	Trimble
Henry Baldwin	1830–1844	Jackson	Washington
James Wayne	1835–1867	Jackson	Johnson
ROGER B. TANEY	1836–1864	Jackson	Marshall
Phillip P. Barbour	1836–1841	Jackson	Duval
John Catron	1837–1865	Jackson	(new judgeship)
John McKinley	1837–1852	Van Buren	(new judgeship)
Peter V. Daniel	1841–1860	Van Buren	Barbour
Samuel Nelson	1845–1872	Tyler	Thompson
Levi Woodbury	1846–1851	Polk	Story
Robert C. Grier	1846–1870	Polk	Baldwin
Benjamin R. Curtis	1851–1857	Fillmore	Woodbury
John A. Campbell	1853–1861	Pierce	McKinley
Nathan Clifford	1858–1881	Buchanan	Curtis
Noah H. Swayne	1862–1881	Lincoln	McLean
Samuel F. Miller	1862–1890	Lincoln	Daniel
David Davis	1862–1877	Lincoln	Campbell
Stephen J. Field	1863–1897	Lincoln	(new judgeship)
SALMON CHASE	1864–1873	Lincoln	Taney
William Strong	1870–1880	Grant	Grier
Joseph P. Bradley	1870–1892	Grant	Wayne
Ward Hunt	1872–1882	Grant	Nelson
MORRISON R. WAITE	1874–1888	Grant	Chase
John Marshall Harlan	1877–1911	Hayes	Davis
William B. Woods	1880–1887	Hayes	Strong
Stanley Matthews	1881–1889	Garfield	Swayne
Horace Gray	1881–1902	Arthur	Clifford
Samuel Blatchford	1882–1893	Arthur	Hunt
Lucius Q. C. Lamar	1888–1893	Cleveland	Woods
MELVILLE W. FULLER	1888–1910	Cleveland	Waite
David J. Brewer	1889–1910	Harrison	Matthews
Henry B. Brown	1890–1906	Harrison	Miller
George Shiras, Jr.	1892–1903	Harrison	Bradley
Howell E. Jackson	1893–1895	Harrison	Lamar

	Tenure	Appointed by	Replaced
Edward D. White	1894–1910	Cleveland	Blatchford
Rufus W. Peckham	1895–1909	Cleveland	Jackson
Joseph McKenna	1898–1925	McKinley	Field
Oliver Wendell Holmes	1902–1932	T. Roosevelt	Gray
William R. Day	1903–1922	T. Roosevelt	Shiras
William H. Moody	1906–1910	T. Roosevelt	Brown
Horace H. Lurton	1909–1914	Taft	Peckham
Charles Evans Hughes	1910–1916	Taft	Brewer
EDWARD D. WHITE	1910–1921	Taft	Fuller
Willis Van Devanter	1910–1937	Taft	White
Joseph R. Lamar	1910–1916	Taft	Moody
Mahlon Pitney	1912–1922	Taft	Harlan
James McReynolds	1914–1941	Wilson	Lurton
Louis D. Brandeis	1916–1939	Wilson	Lamar
John H. Clark	1916–1922	Wilson	Hughes
WILLIAM H. TAFT	1921–1930	Harding	White
George Sutherland	1922–1938	Harding	Clarke
Pierce Butler	1922–1939	Harding	Day
Edward T. Sanford	1923–1930	Harding	Pitney
Harlan F. Stone	1925–1941	Coolidge	McKenna
CHARLES EVANS HUGHES	1930–1941	Hoover	Taft
Owen J. Roberts	1932–1945	Hoover	Sanford
Benjamin N. Cardozo	1932–1938	Hoover	Holmes
Hugo L. Black	1937–1971	F. Roosevelt	Van Devanter
Stanley F. Reed	1938–1957	F. Roosevelt	Sutherland
Felix Frankfurter	1939–1962	F. Roosevelt	Cardozo
William O. Douglas	1939–1975	F. Roosevelt	Brandeis
Frank Murphy	1940–1949	F. Roosevelt	Butler
James F. Byrnes	1941–1942	F. Roosevelt	McReynolds
HARLAN F. STONE	1941–1946	F. Roosevelt	Hughes
Robert H. Jackson	1941–1954	F. Roosevelt	Stone
Wiley B. Rutledge	1943–1949	F. Roosevelt	Byrnes
Harold H. Burton	1945–1958	Truman	Roberts
FRED M. VINSON	1946–1953	Truman	Stone

	Tenure	Appointed by	Replaced
Tom C. Clark	1949–1967	Truman	Murphy
Sherman Minton	1949–1956	Truman	Rutledge
EARL WARREN	1954–1969	Eisenhower	Vinson
John M. Harlan	1955–1971	Eisenhower	Jackson
William J. Brennan	1957–1990	Eisenhower	Minton
Charles E. Whittaker	1957–1962	Eisenhower	Reed
Potter Stewart	1959–1981	Eisenhower	Burton
Byron R. White	1962–1993	Kennedy	Whittaker
Arthur J. Goldberg	1962–1965	Kennedy	Frankfurter
Abe Fortas	1965–1969	Johnson	Goldberg
Thurgood Marshall	1967–1991	Johnson	Clark
WARREN E. BURGER	1969–1986	Nixon	Warren
Harry A. Blackmun	1970–	Nixon	Fortas
Lewis F. Powell	1971–1988	Nixon	Black
William H. Rehnquist	1971–	Nixon	Harlan
John Paul Stevens	1975–	Ford	Douglas
Sandra Day O'Connor	1981–	Reagan	Stewart
WILLIAM H. REHNQUIST	1986–	Reagan	Burger
Antonin Scalia	1986–	Reagan	Rehnquist
Anthony M. Kennedy	1988–	Reagan	Powell
David H. Souter	1990–	Bush	Brennan
Clarence Thomas	1991–	Bush	Marshall
Ruth Bader Ginsburg	1993–	Clinton	White

APPENDIX
C
• • • • • • • • •

A Bill for Establishing Religious Freedom in Virginia

Section I. Well aware that the opinions and belief of men depend on their own will, but follow involuntarily the evidence proposed to their minds; that Almighty God hath created the mind free, and manifested his supreme will that free it shall remain by making it altogether insusceptible of restraint; that all attempts to influence it by temporal punishments, or burthens, or by civil incapacitations, tend only to beget habits of hypocrisy and meanness, and are a departure from the plan of the holy author of our religion, who being lord both of body and mind, yet chose not to propagate it by coercions on either, as was in his Almighty power to do, but to exalt it by its influence on reason alone; that the impious presumption of legislature and ruler, civil as well as ecclesiastical, who, being themselves but fallible and uninspired men, have assumed dominion over the faith of others, setting up their own opinions and modes of thinking as the only true and infallible, and as such endeavoring to impose them on others, hath established and maintained false religions over the greatest part of the world and through all time: That to compel a man to furnish contributions of money for the propagation of opinions which he disbelieves and abhors, is sinful and tyrannical; that even the forcing him to support this or that teacher of his own religious persuasion, is depriving him of the comfortable liberty of giving his contributions to the particular pastor whose morals he would make his pattern, and whose powers he feels most persuasive to righteousness; and is withdrawing from the ministry those temporary rewards, which proceeding from an approbation of their personal conduct, are an additional incitement to earnest and unremitting labours for the instruction of mankind; that our civil rights have no dependence on our religious opinions, any more than our opinions in physics or geometry; and therefore the proscribing any citizen as unworthy the public confidence by laying upon him an incapacity of being called to offices of trust or emolument, unless he profess or renounce this or that religious opinion, is depriving him injudiciously of those privileges and advantages to which, in common with his fellow-citizens, he has a natural right; that it tends also to corrupt the principles of that very religion it is meant to encourage, by bribing with a monopoly of worldly honours and emoluments, those who will externally profess and conform to it; that though indeed these are criminals who do not withstand such temptation, yet neither are those innocent who lay the bait in their way; that the opinions of men are not the object of civil government, nor under its jurisdiction; that to suffer the civil magistrate to intrude his powers into the field of opinion and to restrain the profession or propagation of principles on supposition of their ill tendency is a dangerous fallacy, which at once destroys all religious liberty, because he being of course judge of that tendency will make his opinions the rule of judgment, and approve or condemn the sentiments of others only as they shall square with or suffer from his own; that it is time enough for the rightful purposes of civil government for its officers to interfere when principles break out into overt acts against peace and good order; and finally, that truth is great and will prevail if left to herself; that she is the proper and sufficient antagonist to error, and has nothing to fear from the conflict unless by human interposition disarmed of her natural weapons, free argument and debate; errors ceasing to be dangerous when it is permitted freely to contradict them.

Section II. We the General Assembly of Virginia do enact that no man shall be compelled to frequent or support any religious worship, place, or ministry whatsoever, nor shall be enforced, restrained, molested, or burthened in his body or goods, or shall otherwise suffer, on account of his religious opinions or belief; but that all men shall be free to profess, and by argument to maintain, their opinions in matters of religion, and that the same shall in no wise diminish, enlarge, or affect their civil capacities.

Section III. And though we well know that this Assembly, elected by the people for their ordinary purposes of legislation only, have no power to restrain the acts of succeeding Assemblies, constituted with powers equal to our own, and that therefore to declare this act to be irrevocable would be of no effect in law; yet we are free to declare, and do declare, that the rights hereby asserted are of the natural rights of mankind, and that if any act shall be hereafter passed to repeal the present or to narrow its operations, such act will be an infringement of natural right.

INDEX

✸ ✸ ✸ ✸ ✸ ✸ ✸ ✸

by Darien A. McWhirter